Sir Gawayne

and

The Green Knight.

Sir Gawayne

and

The Green Knight:

AN ALLITERATIVE ROMANCE-POEM,

(AB. 1320-30 A.D.)

BY THE AUTHOR OF

EARLY ENGLISH ALLITERATIVE POEMS.

RE-EDITED FROM COTTON. MS. NERO, A. X., IN THE BRITISH MUSEUM,

BY

RICHARD MORRIS,

EDITOR OF HAMPOLE'S "PRICKE OF CONSCIENCE," "EARLY ENGLISH ALLITERATIVE POEMS," ETC.;
MEMBER OF THE COUNCIL OF THE PHILOLOGICAL SOCIETY.

G. E. STECHERT & CO's REPRINT OF RARE BOOKS.

1917.

PREFACE.

In re-editing the present romance-poem I have been saved all labour of transcription by using the very accurate text contained in Sir F. Madden's "Syr Gawayne."

I have not only read his copy with the manuscript, but also the proof-sheets as they came to hand, hoping by this means to give the reader a text free from any errors of transcription.

The present edition differs from that of the earlier one in having the contractions of the manuscript expanded and side-notes added to the text to enable the reader to follow with some degree of ease the author's pleasant narrative of Sir Gawayne's adventures.

The Glossary is taken from Sir F. Madden's "Syr Gawayne,"[1] to which, for the better interpretation of the text, I have made several additions, and have, moreover, glossed nearly all the words previously left unexplained.

For a description of the Manuscript, and particulars relating to the authorship and dialect of the present work, the reader is referred to the preface to *Early English Alliterative Poems*.

R. M.

London,
December 22, 1864.

[1] Sir F. Madden has most generously placed at the disposal of the Early English Text Society any of his works which it may determine to re-edit.

b

CORRECTIONS.

Page 50, l. 1583, dele the comma after *leue*.

Page 63, l. 1991, for *soundly* read *soundyly*.

Page 78, l. 2461, for *gomen* (*sic* MS.) read *gome*.

Page 109, col. 2, l. 44 (Glossary) ; dele the interpretation of *Pese*, and substitute the following :—

Pese=*pease* (pisum) ; *quite pease*='white pease.'

" Set shallow brooks to surging seas,
An Orient pearl to a *white pease*.""

(Puttenham, quoted by Trench—*English, Past and Present*, p. 162.)

INTRODUCTION.

No Knight of the Round Table has been so highly honoured by the old Romance writers as Sir Gawayne the son of Loth, and nephew to the renowned Arthur. They delighted to describe him as Gawayne the good, a man matchless on mould, the most gracious that under God lived, the hardiest of hard, the most fortunate in arms, and the most polite in hall, whose knowledge, knighthood, kindly works, doings, doughtiness, and deeds of arms were known in all lands.

When Arthur beheld the dead body of his kinsman lying on the ground bathed in blood, he is said to have exclaimed, "O righteous God, this blood were worthy to be preserved and enshrined in gold!" Our author, too, loves to speak of his hero in similar terms of praise, calling him the knight faultless in his five wits, void of every offence, and adorned with every earthly virtue. He represents him as one whose trust was in the five wounds, and in whom the five virtues which distinguished the true knight were more firmly established than in any other on earth.

The author of the present story, who, as we know from his religious poems, had an utter horror of moral impurity, could have chosen no better subject for a romance in which amusement and moral instruction were to be combined. In the following tale he shows how the true knight, though tempted sorely not once alone, but twice, nay thrice, breaks not his vow of chastity, but turns aside the tempter's shafts with the shield of purity and arm of faith, and so passes scatheless through the perilous defile of trial and opportunity seeming safe.

But while our author has borrowed many of the details of his story from the "Roman de Perceval" by Chrestien de Troyes, he has made the narrative more attractive by the introduction of several original and highly interesting passages which throw light on the manners and amusements of our ancestors.

The following elaborate descriptions are well deserving of especial notice:—

I. The mode of completely arming a knight (p. 18).

II. The hunting and breaking the deer (pp. 36–42).

III. The hunting and unlacing the wild boar (pp. 45–50).

IV. A fox hunt (pp. 54–61).

The following is an outline of the story of Gawayne's adventures, more or less in the words of the writer himself :—

Arthur, the greatest of Britain's kings, holds the Christmas festival at Camelot, surrounded by the celebrated knights of the Round Table, noble lords, the most renowned under heaven, and ladies the loveliest that ever had life (p. 2). This noble company celebrate the New Year by a religious service, by the bestowal of gifts, and the most joyous mirth. Lords and ladies take their seats at the table—Queen Guenever, the grey-eyed, gaily dressed, sits at the daïs, the high table, or table of state, where too sat Gawayne and Ywain together with other worthies of the Round Table (p. 3). Arthur, in mood as joyful as a child, his blood young and his brain wild, declares that he will not eat nor sit long at the table until some adventurous thing, some uncouth tale, some great marvel, or some encounter of arms has occurred to mark the return of the New Year (p. 4).

The first course was announced with cracking of trumpets, with the noise of nakers and noble pipes.

> " Each two had dishes twelve,
> Good beer and bright wine both."

Scarcely was the first course served when another noise than that of music was heard. There rushes in at the hall-door a knight of gigantic stature—the greatest on earth—in measure high. He was clothed entirely in green, and rode upon a green foal (p. 5). Fair wavy hair fell about the shoulders of the Green Knight, and a great beard like a bush hung upon his breast (p. 6).

The knight carried no helmet, shield, or spear, but in one hand a holly bough, and in the other an axe "huge and unmeet," the edge of which was as keen as a sharp razor (p. 7). Thus arrayed, the Green Knight enters the hall without saluting any one. The first word that he uttered was, "Where is the governour of this gang, gladly would I see him and with himself speak reason." To the knights he cast his eye, looking for the most renowned. Much did the noble assembly marvel to see a man and a horse of such a hue, green as the grass. Even greener they seemed than green enamel on bright gold. Many marvels had they seen, but none such as this. They were afraid to answer, but sat stone still in a dead silence, as if overpowered by sleep.

"Not all from fear, but some for courtesy" (p. 8).

Then Arthur before the high daïs salutes the Green Knight, bids him welcome, and entreats him to stay awhile at his Court. The knight says that his errand is not to abide in any dwelling, but to seek the most valiant of the heroes of the Round Table that he may put his courage to the proof, and thus satisfy himself as to the fame of Arthur's court. "I come," he says, "in peace, as ye may see by this branch that I bear here. Had I come with hostile intentions, I should not have left my hauberk, helmet, shield, sharp spear, and other weapons behind me. But because I desire no war, 'my weeds are softer.' If thou be so bold as all men say, thou wilt grant me the request I am about to make." "Sir courteous knight," replies Arthur, "if thou cravest battle only, here failest thou not to fight." "Nay," says the Green Knight, "I seek no fighting. Here about on this bench are only beardless children. Were I arrayed in arms, on a high steed, no man here would be a match for me (p. 9). But it is now Christmas time, and this is the New Year, and I see around me many brave ones;—if any be so bold in his blood that dare strike a stroke for another, I shall give him this rich axe to do with it whatever he pleases. I shall abide the first blow just as I sit, and will stand him a stroke, stiff on this floor, provided that I deal him another in return.

'And yet give I him respite,
A twelvemonth and a day ;
Now haste and let see tite (soon)
Dare any here-in ought say.'"

If he astounded them at first, much more so did he after this speech, and fear held them all silent. The knight, righting himself in his saddle, rolls fiercely his red eyes about, bends his bristly green brows, and strokes his beard awaiting a reply. But finding none that would carp with him, he exclaims, "What! is this Arthur's house, the fame of which has spread through so many realms? Forsooth, the renown of the Round Table is overturned by the word of one man's speech, for all tremble for dread without a blow being struck!" (p. 10). With this he laughed so loud that Arthur blushed for very shame, and waxed as wroth as the wind. "I know no man," he says, "that is aghast at thy great words. Give me now thy axe and I will grant thee thy request!" Arthur seizes the axe, grasps the handle, and sternly brandishes it about, while the Green Knight, with a stern cheer and a dry countenance, stroking his beard and drawing down his coat, awaits the blow (p. 11). Sir Gawayne, the nephew of the king, beseeches his uncle to let him undertake the encounter; and, at the earnest entreaty of his nobles, Arthur consents "to give Gawayne the game" (p. 12).

Sir Gawayne then takes possession of the axe, but, before the blow is dealt, the Green Knight asks the name of his opponent. "In good faith," answers the good knight, "Gawayne I am called, that bids thee to this buffet, whatever may befall after, and at this time twelvemonth will take from thee another, with whatever weapon thou wilt, and with no wight else alive." "By Gog," quoth the Green Knight, "it pleases me well that I shall receive at thy fist that which I have sought here—moreover thou hast truly rehearsed the terms of the covenant,—but thou shalt first pledge me thy word that thou wilt seek me thyself, wheresoever on earth thou believest I may be found, and fetch thee such wages as thou dealest me to-day before this company of doughty ones." "Where should I seek thee?" replies Gawayne, "where is thy place? I know not thee, thy court, or thy name. I wot not where thou dwellest, but teach me thereto, tell me how thou art called, and I shall endeavour to find thee,—and that I swear thee for truth and by my sure troth." "That is enough in New Year," says the groom in green, "if I tell thee when I have received the tap. When thou hast smitten me, then smartly I will teach thee of my house, my home, and my own name, so that thou mayest follow my track and fulfil the covenant between us. If I spend no speech, then speedest thou the better, for then mayest thou remain in thy own land and seek no further; but cease thy talking[1] (p 13). Take now thy grim tool to thee and let us see how thou knockest." "Gladly, sir, for sooth," quoth Gawayne, and his axe he brandishes.

The Green Knight adjusts himself on the ground, bends slightly his head, lays his long lovely locks over his crown, and lays bare his neck for the blow. Gawayne then gripped the axe, and, raising it on high, let it fall quickly upon the knight's neck and severed the head from the body. The fair head fell from the neck to the earth, and many turned it aside with their feet as it rolled forth. The blood burst from the body, yet the knight never faltered nor fell; but boldly he started forth on stiff shanks and fiercely rushed forward, seized his head, and lifted it up quickly. Then he runs to his horse, the bridle he catches, steps into his saddle and strides aloft. His head by the hair he holds in his hands, and sits as firmly in his saddle as if no mishap had ailed

---

[1] This, I think, is the true explanation of *slokes.*

him, though headless he was (p. 14). He turned his ugly trunk about —that ugly body that bled,—and holding the head in his hand, he directed the face toward the "dearest on the dais." The head lifted up its eyelids and looked abroad, and thus much spoke with its mouth as ye may now hear :—

"Loke, Gawayne, thou be prompt to go as thou hast promised, and seek till thou find me according to thy promise made in the hearing of these knights. Get thee to the Green Chapel, I charge thee, to fetch such a dint as thou hast dealt, to be returned on New Year's morn. As the Knight of the Green Chapel I am known to many, wherefore if thou seekest thou canst not fail to find me. Therefore come, or recreant be called." With a fierce start the reins he turns, rushes out of the hall-door, his head in his hand, so that the fire of the flint flew from the hoofs of his foal. To what kingdom he belonged knew none there, nor knew they from whence he had come. What then?

> "The king and Gawayne there
> At that green (one) they laugh and grin."

Though Arthur wondered much at the marvel, he let no one see that he was at all troubled about it, but full loudly thus spake to his comely queen with courteous speech :

"Dear dame, to-day be never dismayed, well happens such craft at Christmas time. I may now proceed to meat, for I cannot deny that I have witnessed a wondrous adventure this day" (p. 15).

He looked upon Sir Gawayne and said, "Now sir, hang up thine axe, for enough has it hewn." So the weapon was hung up on high that all might look upon it, and "by true title thereof tell the wonder." Then all the knights hastened to their seats at the table, so did the king and our good knight, and they were there served with all dainties, "with all manner of meat and minstrelsy."

Though words were wanting when they first to seat went, now are their hands full of stern work, and the marvel affords them good subject for conversation. But a year passes full quickly and never returns,—the beginning is seldom like the end ; wherefore this Christmas passed away and the year after, and each season in turn followed after another (p. 16). Thus winter winds round again, and then Gawayne thinks of his wearisome journey (p. 17). On All-hallows day Arthur entertains right nobly the lords and ladies of his court in honour of his nephew, for whom all courteous knights and lovely ladies were in great grief. Nevertheless they spoke only of mirth, and, though joyless themselves, made many a joke to cheer the good Sir Gawayne (p. 18). Early on the morrow Sir Gawayne, with great ceremony, is arrayed in his armour (p. 19), and thus completely equipped for his adventure he first hears mass, and afterwards takes leave of Arthur, the knights of the Round Table, and the lords and ladies of the court, who kiss him and commend him to Christ. He bids them all good day, as he thought, for evermore (p. 21);

"Very much was the warm water that poured from eyes that day."

Now rides our knight through the realms of England with no companion but his foal, and no one to hold converse with save God alone. From Camelot, in Somersetshire, he proceeds through Gloucestershire and the adjoining counties into Montgomeryshire, and thence through North Wales to Holyhead, adjoining the Isle of Anglesea (p. 22), from which he passes into the very narrow peninsula of Wirral, in Cheshire, where dwelt but few that loved God or man. Gawayne enquires after the Green Knight of the Green Chapel, but all the inhabitants declare that they had never seen "any man of such hues of green."

The knight thence pursues his journey by strange paths, over hill and moor, encountering on his way not only serpents, wolves, bulls, bears, and boars, but wood satyrs and giants. But worse than all these, however, was the sharp winter, "when the cold clear water shed from the clouds, and froze ere it might fall to the earth. Nearly slain with the sleet he slept in his armour, more nights than enough, in naked rocks" (p. 23).

Thus in peril and plight the knight travels on until Christmas-eve, and to Mary he makes his moan that she may direct him to some abode. On the morn he arrives at an immense forest, wondrously wild, surrounded by high hills on every side, where he found hoary oaks full huge, a hundred together. The hazel and the hawthorn intermingled were all overgrown with moss, and upon their boughs sat many sad birds that piteously piped for pain of the cold. Gawayne besought the Lord and Mary to guide him to some habitation where he might hear mass (p. 24). Scarcely had he crossed himself thrice, when he perceived a dwelling in the wood set upon a hill. It was the loveliest castle he had ever beheld. It was pitched on a prairie, with a park all about it, enclosing many a tree for more than two miles. It shone as the sun through the bright oaks (p. 25).

Gawayne urges on his steed Gringolet, and finds himself at the "chief gate." He called aloud, and soon there appeared a "porter" on the wall, who demanded his errand.

"Good sir," quoth Gawayne, "wouldst thou go to the high lord of this house, and crave a lodging for me?"

"Yea, by Peter!" replied the porter, "well I know that thou art welcome to dwell here as long as thou likest."

The drawbridge is soon let down, and the gates opened wide to receive the knight. Many noble ones hasten to bid him welcome (p. 26). They take away his helmet, sword, and shield, and many a proud one presses forward to do him honour. They bring him into the hall, where a fire was brightly burning upon the hearth. Then the lord of the land[1] comes from his chamber and welcomes Sir Gawayne, telling him that he is to consider the place as his own. Our knight is next

---

[1] Gawayne is now in the castle of the Green Knight, who, divested of his elvish or supernatural character, appears to our knight merely as a bold one with a beaver-hued beard.

conducted to a bright bower, where was noble bedding—curtains of pure silk, with golden hems, and Tarsic tapestries upon the walls and the floors (p. 27). Here the knight doffed his armour and put on rich robes, which so well became him, that all declared that a more comely knight Christ had never made (p. 28).

A table is soon raised, and Gawayne, having washed, proceeds to meat. Many dishes are set before him—"sews" of various kinds, fish of all kinds, some baked in bread, others broiled on the embers, some boiled, and others seasoned with spices. The knight expresses himself well pleased, and calls it a most noble and princely feast.

After dinner he, in reply to numerous questions, tells his host that he is Gawayne, one of the Knights of the Round Table. When this was made known great was the joy in the hall. Each one said softly to his companion, "Now we shall see courteous behaviour and learn the terms of noble discourse, since we have amongst us 'that fine father of nurture.' Truly God has highly favoured us in sending us such a noble guest as Sir Gawayne" (p. 29). At the end of the Christmas festival Gawayne desires to take his departure from the castle, but his host persuades him to stay, promising to direct him to the Green Chapel (about two miles from the chapel), that he may be there by the appointed time (p. 34).

A covenant is made between them, the terms of which were that the lord of the castle should go out early to the chase, that Gawayne meanwhile should lie in his loft at his ease, then rise at his usual hour, and afterwards sit at table with his hostess, and that at the end of the day they should make an exchange of whatever they might obtain in the interim. "Whatever I win in the wood," says the lord, "shall be yours, and what thou gettest shall be mine" (p. 35).

Full early before daybreak the folk uprise, saddle their horses, and truss their mails. The noble lord of the land, arrayed for riding, eats hastily a sop, and having heard mass, proceeds with a hundred hunters to hunt the wild deer (p. 36).

All this time Gawayne lies in his gay bed. His nap is disturbed by a little noise at the door, which is softly opened. He heaves up his head out of the clothes, and, peeping through the curtains, beholds a most lovely lady (the wife of his host). She came towards the bed, and the knight laid himself down quickly, pretending to be asleep. The lady stole to the bed, cast up the curtains, crept within, sat her softly on the bed-side, and waited some time till the knight should awake. After lurking awhile under the clothes considering what it all meant, Gawayne unlocked his eyelids, and put on a look of surprise, at the same time making the sign of the cross, as if afraid of some hidden danger (p. 38). "Good morrow, sir," said that fair lady, "ye are a careless sleeper to let one enter thus. I shall bind you in your bed, of that be ye sure." "Good morrow," quoth Gawayne, "I shall act according to your will with great pleasure, but permit me to rise that I may the more comfortably converse with you." "Nay, beau sir," said that sweet one, "ye shall not rise from your bed, for since I have caught my knight I shall hold talk with him. I ween well that ye are Sir Gawayne that all the world worships, whose honour and courtesy are so greatly praised. Now ye are here, and we are alone (my lord and his men being afar off, other men, too, are in bed, so are my maidens), and the door is safely closed, I shall use my time well while it lasts. Ye are welcome to my person to do with it as ye please, and I will be your servant " (p. 39).

Gawayne behaves most discreetly, for the remembrance of his forth-coming adventure at the Green Chapel prevents him from thinking of love (p. 41). At last the lady takes leave of the knight by catching him in her arms and kissing him (p. 41). The day passes away merrily, and at dusk the lord of the castle returns from the chase. He presents the veni-son to Gawayne according to the previous covenant between them. Our knight gives his host a kiss as the only piece of good fortune that had fallen to him during the day. "It is good," says the other, "and would be much better if ye would tell me where ye won such bliss" (p. 44). "That was not in our covenant," replies Gawayne, "so try me no more." After much laughing on both sides they proceed to supper, and afterwards, while the choice wine is being carried round, Gawayne and his host renew their agreement. Late at night they take leave of each other and hasten to their beds. "By the time that the cock had crowed and cackled thrice" the lord was up, and after "meat and mass" were over the hunters make for the woods, where they give chase to a wild boar who had grown old and mischievous (p. 45).

While the sportsmen are hunting this "wild swine" our lovely knight lies in his bed. He is not forgotten by the lady, who pays him an early visit, seeking to make further trial of his virtues. She sits softly by his side and tells him that he has forgotten what she taught him the day before (p. 47). " I taught you of kissing," says she ; "that becomes every courteous knight." Gawayne says that he must not take that which is forbidden him. The lady replies that he is strong enough to enforce his own wishes. Our knight answers that every gift not given with a good will is worthless. His fair visitor then enquires how it is that he who is so skilled in the true sport of love and so renowned a knight, has never talked to her of love (p. 48). "You ought," she says, "to show and teach a young thing like me some tokens of true-love's crafts; I come hither and sit here alone to learn of you some game; do teach me of your wit while my lord is from home." Gawayne replies that he cannot undertake the task of ex-pounding true-love and tales of arms to one who has far more wisdom than he possesses. Thus did our knight avoid all appearance of evil, though sorely pressed to do what was wrong (p. 49). The lady, having bestowed two kisses upon Sir Gawayne, takes her leave of him (p. 50).

At the end of the day the lord of the castle returns home with the shields and head of the wild boar. He shows them to his guest, who declares that "such a brawn of a beast, nor such sides of a swine," he never before has seen. Gawayne takes possession of the spoil according to covenant, and in return he bestows two kisses upon his host, who declares that his guest has indeed been rich with "such chaffer" (p. 52).

After much persuasion, Gawayne consents to stop at the castle another day (p. 53). Early on the morrow the lord and his men hasten to the woods, and come upon the track of a fox, the hunting of which affords them plenty of employment and sport (p. 54). Meanwhile our good knight sleeps soundly within his comely curtains. He is again visited by the lady of the castle. So gaily was she attired, and so "faultless of her features," that great joy warmed the heart of Sir Gawayne. With soft and pleasant smiles "they smite into mirth," and are soon engaged in conversation. Had not Mary thought of her knight, he would have been in great peril (p. 56). So sorely does the fair one press him with her love, that he fears lest he should become a traitor to his host. The lady enquires whether he has a mistress to whom he has plighted his troth. The knight swears by St. John that he neither has nor desires one. This answer causes the dame to sigh for sorrow, and telling him that she must depart, she asks for some gift, if it were only a glove, by which she might "think on the knight and lessen her grief" (p. 57). Gawayne assures her that he has nothing worthy of her acceptance; that he is on an "uncouth errand," and therefore has "no men with no mails containing precious things," for which he is truly sorry.

Quoth that lovesome (one)—

"Though I had nought of yours,
Yet should ye have of mine."

Thus saying, she offers him a rich ring of red gold "with a shining stone standing aloft," that shone like the beams of the bright sun. The knight refused the gift, as he had nothing to give in return. "Since ye refuse my ring," says the lady, "because it seems too rich, and ye would not be beholden to me, I shall give you my girdle that is less valuable" (p. 58). But Gawayne replies that he will not accept gold or a reward of any kind, though "ever in hot and in cold" he will be her true servant.

"Do you refuse it," asks the lady, "because it seems simple and of little value? Whoso knew the virtues that are knit therein would estimate it more highly. For he who is girded with this green lace cannot be wounded or slain by any man under heaven." The knight thinks awhile, and it strikes him that this would be "jewel for the jeopardy" that he had to undergo at the Green Chapel. So he not only accepts the lace, but promises to keep the possession of it a secret (p. 59). By that time the lady had kissed him thrice, and she then takes "her leave and leaves him there."

Gawayne rises, dresses himself in noble array, and conceals the "love lace" where he might find it again. He then hies to mass, shrives him of his misdeeds, and obtains absolution. On his return to the hall he solaces the ladies with comely carols and all kinds of joy (p. 60). The dark night came, and then the lord of the castle, having slain the

fox, returns to his "dear home," where he finds a fire brightly burning
and his guest amusing the ladies (p. 61). Gawayne, in fulfilment of his
agreement, kisses his host thrice.[1] "By Christ," quoth the other knight,
"ye have caught much bliss. I have hunted all this day and nought
have I got but the skin of this foul fox (the devil have the goods), and
that is full poor for to pay for such precious things" (p. 62).

After the usual evening's entertainment, Gawayne retires to rest.
The next morning, being New Year's day, is cold and stormy. Snow
falls, and the dales are full of drift. Our knight in his bed locks his
eyelids, but full little he sleeps. By each cock that crows he knows
the hour, and before day-break he calls for his chamberlain, who
quickly brings him his armour (p. 64). While Gawayne clothed himself
in his rich weeds he forgot not the "lace, the lady's gift," but with it
doubly girded his loins. He wore it not for its rich ornaments, "but
to save himself when it behoved him to suffer," and as a safeguard
against sword or knife (p. 65).

Having thanked his host and all the renowned assembly for the great
kindness he had experienced at their hands, "he steps into stirrups
and strides aloft" (p. 66).

The drawbridge is let down, and the broad gates unbarred and
borne open upon both sides, and the knight, after commending the castle
to Christ, passes thereout and goes on his way accompanied by his
guide, that should teach him to turn to that place where he should
receive the much dreaded blow. They climb over cliffs, where each
hill had a hat and a mist-cloak, until the next morn, when they find
themselves on a full high hill covered with snow. The servant bids
his master remain awhile, saying, "I have brought you hither at this
time, and now ye are not far from that noted place that ye have so
often enquired after. The place that ye press to is esteemed full
perilous, and there dwells a man in that waste the worst upon earth,
for he is stiff and stern and loves to strike, and greater is he than any
man upon middle-earth, and his body is bigger than the best four in
Arthur's house. He keeps the Green Chapel; there passes none by
that place, however proud in arms, that he does not 'ding him to
death with dint of his hand.' He is a man immoderate and 'no mercy
uses,' for be it churl or chaplain that by the chapel rides, monk or
mass-priest, or any man else, it is as pleasant to him to kill them as to
go alive himself. Wherefore I tell thee truly, 'come ye there, ye be
killed, though ye had twenty lives to spend. He has dwelt there long
of yore, and on field much sorrow has wrought. Again his dints sore
ye may not defend you' (p. 67). Therefore, good Sir Gawayne, let the man
alone, and for God's sake go by some other path, and then I shall hie
me home again. I swear to you by God and all His saints that I will
never say that ever ye attempted to flee from any man."

Gawayne thanks his guide for his well-meant kindness, but declares

---

[1] He only in part keeps to his covenant, as he holds back the *love-lace*.

that to the Green Chapel he will go, though the owner thereof be "a stern knave," for God can devise means to save his servants.

"Mary!" quoth the other, "since it pleases thee to lose thy life, I will not hinder thee. Have thy helmet on thy head, thy spear in thy hand, and ride down this path by yon rock-side, till thou be brought to the bottom of the valley. Then look a little on the plain, on thy left hand, and thou shalt see in that slade the chapel itself, and the burly knight that guards it (p. 68). Now, farewell Gawayne the noble! for all the gold upon ground I would not go with thee nor bear thee fellowship through this wood 'on foot farther.'" Thus having spoken, he gallops away and leaves the knight alone.

Gawayne now pursues his journey, rides through the dale, and looks about. He sees no signs of a resting-place, but only high and steep banks, and the very shadows of the high woods seemed wild and distorted. No chapel, however, could he discover. After a while he sees a round hill by the side of a stream; thither he goes, alights, and fastens his horse to the branch of a tree. He walks about the hill, debating with himself what it might be. It had a hole in the one end and on each side, and everywhere overgrown with grass, but whether it was only an old cave or a crevice of an old crag he could not tell (p. 69).

"Now, indeed," quoth Gawayne, "a desert is here; this oratory is ugly with herbs overgrown. It is a fitting place for the man in green to 'deal here his devotions after the devil's manner.' Now I feel it is the fiend (the devil) in my five wits that has covenanted with me that he may destroy me. This is a chapel of misfortune—evil betide it! It is the most cursed kirk that ever I came in." With his helmet on his head, and spear in his hand, he roams up to the rock, and then he hears from that high hill beyond the brook a wondrous wild noise. Lo! it clattered in the cliff as if one upon a grindstone were grinding a scythe. It whirred like the water at a mill, and rushed and re-echoed, terrible to hear. "Though my life I forego," says Gawayne, "no noise shall cause me to fear."

Then he cried aloud, "Who dwells in this place, discourse with me to hold? For now is good Gawayne going right here if any brave wight will hie him hither, either now or never" (p. 70).

"Abide," quoth one on the bank above, over his head, "and thou shalt have all in haste that I promised thee once."

Soon there comes out of a hole in the crag, with a fell weapon, a Danish axe quite new, the "man in the green," clothed as at first as to his legs, locks, and beard. But now he is on foot and walks on the earth. When he reaches the stream, he hops over and boldly strides about. He meets Sir Gawayne, who tells him that he is quite ready to fulfil his part of the compact. "Gawayne," quoth that 'green gome' (man), "may God preserve thee! Truly thou art welcome to my place, 'and thou hast timed thy travel' as a true man should. Thou knowest the covenants made between us, at this time twelve.

month, that on New Year's day I should return thee thy blow. We are now in this valley by ourselves, and can do as we please (p. 71). Have, therefore, thy helmet off thy head, and 'have here thy pay.' Let us have no more talk than when thou didst strike off my head with a single blow."

"Nay, by God!" quoth Gawayne, "I shall not begrudge thee thy will for any harm that may happen, but will stand still while thou strikest."

Then he stoops a little and shows his bare neck, unmoved by any fear. The Green Knight takes up his "grim tool," and with all his force raises it aloft, as if he meant utterly to destroy him. As the axe came gliding down Gawayne "shrank a little with the shoulders from the sharp iron." The other withheld his weapon, and then reproved the prince with many proud words. "Thou art not Gawayne that is so good esteemed, that never feared for no host by hill nor by vale, for now thou fleest for fear before thou feelest harm (p. 72). Such cowardice of that knight did I never hear. I never flinched nor fled when thou didst aim at me in King Arthur's house. My head flew to my feet and yet I never fled, wherefore I deserve to be called the better man."

Quoth Gawayne, "I shunted once, but will do so no more, though my head fall on the stones. But hasten and bring me to the point; deal me my destiny, and do it out of hand, for I shall stand thee a stroke and start no more until thine axe has hit me—have here my troth." "Have at thee, then," said the other, and heaves the axe aloft, and looks as savagely as if he were mad. He aims at the other mightily, but withholds his hand ere it might hurt. Gawayne readily abides the blow without flinching with any member, and stood still as a stone or a tree fixed in rocky ground with a hundred roots.

Then merrily the other did speak, "Since now thou hast thy heart whole it behoves me to strike, so take care of thy neck." Gawayne answers with great wroth, "Thrash on, thou fierce man, thou threatenest too long; I believe thy own heart fails thee."

"Forsooth," quoth the other, since thou speakest so boldly, I will no longer delay" (p. 73). Then, contracting "both lips and brow," he made ready to strike, and let fall his axe on the bare neck of Sir Gawayne. "Though he hammered" fiercely, he only "severed the hide," causing the blood to flow. When Gawayne saw his blood on the snow, he quickly seized his helmet and placed it on his head. Then he drew out his bright sword, and thus angrily spoke: "Cease, man, of thy blow, bid me no more. I have received a stroke in this place without opposition, but if thou givest me any more readily shall I requite thee, of that be thou sure. Our covenant stipulates one stroke, and therefore now cease."

The Green Knight, resting on his axe, looks on Sir Gawayne, as bold and fearless he there stood, and then with a loud voice thus addresses the knight: "Bold knight, be not so wroth, no man here has wronged thee (p. 74); I promised thee a stroke, and thou hast it, so hold thee well pleased. I could have dealt much worse with thee, and caused thee much sorrow. Two blows I aimed at thee, for twice thou kissedst my fair wife; but I struck thee not, because thou restoredst them to me according to agreement. At the third time thou failedst, and therefore I have given thee that tap. That woven girdle, given thee by my own wife, belongs to me. I know well thy kisses, thy conduct also, and the wooing of my wife, for I wrought it myself. I sent her to try thee, and truly methinks thou art the most faultless man that ever on foot went. Still, sir, thou we.t wanting in good faith; but as it proceeded from no immorality, thou being only desirous of saving thy life, the less I blame thee."

Gawayne stood confounded, the blood rushed into his face, and he shrank within himself for very shame. "Cursed," he cried, "be cowardice and covetousness both; in you are villany and vice, that virtue destroy." Then he takes off the girdle and throws it to the knight in green, cursing his cowardice and covetousness. The Green Knight, laughing, thus spoke: "Thou hast confessed so clean, and acknowledged thy faults, that I hold thee as pure as thou hadst never forfeited since thou wast first born. I give thee, sir, the gold-hemmed girdle as a token of thy adventure at the Green Chapel. Come now to my castle, and we shall enjoy together the festivities of the New Year" (p. 76).

"Nay, forsooth," quoth the knight, "but for your kindness may God requite you. Commend me to that courteous one your comely wife, who with her crafts has beguiled me. But it is no uncommon thing for a man to come to sorrow through women's wiles; for so was Adam beguiled with one, and Solomon with many. Samson was destroyed by Delilah, and David suffered much through Bathsheba. '*It were indeed great bliss for a man to love them well and believe them not.*' Since the greatest upon earth were so beguiled, methinks I should be excused. But God reward you for your girdle, which I will ever wear in remembrance of my fault, and when pride shall exalt me, a look to this love-lace shall lessen it (p. 77). But since ye are the lord of yonder land, from whom I have received so much honour, tell me truly your right name, and I shall ask no more questions."

Quoth the other, "I am called Bernlak de Hautdesert, through might of Morgain la Fay, who dwells in my house. Much has she learnt of Merlin, who knows all your knights at home. She brought me to your hall for to essay the prowess of the Round Table. She wrought this wonder to bereave you of your wits, hoping to have grieved Guenever and affrighted her to death by means of the man that spoke with his head in his hand before the high table. She is even thine aunt, Arthur's half sister; wherefore come to thine aunt, for all my household love thee."

Gawayne refuses to accompany the Green Knight, and so, with many embraces and kind wishes, they separate—the one to his castle, the other to Arthur's court.

After passing through many wild ways, our knight recovers from the wound in his neck, and at last comes safe and sound to the court of King Arthur. Great then was the joy of all; the king and queen kiss their brave knight, and make many enquiries about his journey. He tells them of his adventures, hiding nothing—"the chance of the chapel, the cheer of the knight, the love of the lady, and lastly of the lace." Groaning for grief and shame he shows them the cut in his neck, which he had received for his unfaithfulness (p. 79). The king and his courtiers comfort the knight—they laugh loudly at his adventures, and unanimously agree that those lords and ladies that belonged to the Round Table, and each knight of the brotherhood, should ever after wear a bright green belt for Gawayne's sake. And he upon whom it was conferred honoured it evermore after.

Thus in Arthur's time this adventure befell, whereof the "Brutus Books" bear witness (p. 80).

I need not say that the *Brutus Books* we possess do not contain the legend here set forth, though it is not much more improbable than some of the statements contained in them. If the reader desires to know the relation in which this and the like stories stand to the original Arthur legends, he will find it discussed in Sir F. Madden's Preface to his edition of "Syr Gawayne," which also contains a sketch of the very different views taken of Sir Gawayne by the different Romance writers.

Into this and other *literary* questions I do not enter here, as I have nothing to add to Sir F. Madden's statements; but in the text of the Poem I have differed from him in some few readings, which will be found noticed in the Notes and Glossary.

As the manuscript is fast fading, I am glad that the existence of the Early English Text Society has enabled us to secure a wider diffusion of its contents before the original shall be no longer legible.

We want nothing but an increased supply of members to enable us to give to a large circle of readers many an equally interesting record of Early English minds.

SYR GAWAYN AND THE GRENE KNYȜT.

[FYTTE THE FIRST.]

I.

SIþEN þe sege & þe assaut watȝ sesed at Troye,   [Fol. 91a.]
    þe borȝ brittened & brent to brondeȝ & askeȝ,   After the siege of
                                        Troy
    þe tulk þat þe trammes of tresoun þer wroȝt,
4 Watȝ tried for his tricherie, þe trewest on erthe;
    Hit watȝ Ennias þe athel, & his highe kynde,
    þat siþen depreced prouinces, & patroúnes bicome
    Welneȝe of al þe wele in þe west iles,
8 Fro riche Romulus to Rome ricchis hym swyþe,   Romulus built
    With gret bobbaunce þat burȝe he biges vpon fyrst, Rome,
    & neuenes hit his aune nome, as hit now hat;
    Ticius to Tuskan [turnes,] & teldes bigynnes;
12 Langaberde in Lumbardie lyftes vp homes;
    & fer ouer þe French flod Felix Brutus   and Felix Brutus
    On mony bonkkes ful brode Bretayn he setteȝ, founded Britain,
               wyth wynne;
16   Where werre, & wrake, & wonder,   a land of war and
       Bi syþeȝ hatȝ wont þer-inne,   wonder,
       & oft boþe blysse & blunder   and oft of bliss
       Ful skete hatȝ skyfted synne.   and blunder.

II.

20 Ande quen þis Bretayn watȝ bigged bi þis burn ryoh,
    Bolde bredden þer-inne, baret þat lofden,   Bold men in-
    In mony turned tyme tene þat wroȝten;   creased in the
    Mo ferlyes on þis folde han fallen here oft   land,

1

24   Þen in any oþer þat I wot, syn þat ilk tyme.

Bot of alle þat here bult of Bretaygne kynges

Ay watȝ Arthur þe hendest, as I haf herde telle;

For-þi an aunter in erde I attle to schawe,

28   Þat a selly in siȝt summe men hit holden,

& an outtrage awenture of Arthureȝ wondereȝ;

If ȝe wyl lysten þis laye bot on littel quile,

I schal telle hit, as-tit, as I in toun herde,

32   with tonge;

As hit is stad & stoken,

In stori stif & stronge,

With lel letteres loken,

36   In londe so hatȝ ben longe.

III.

Þis kyng lay at Camylot vpon kryst-masse,

With mony luflych lorde, ledeȝ of þe best,

Rekenly of þe rounde table alle þo rich breþer,

40   With rych reuel oryȝt, & rechles merþes;

Þer tournayed tulkes bi-tymeȝ ful mony,

Iusted ful Iolilé þise gentyle kniȝtes,

Syþen kayred to þe court, caroles to make.

44   For þer þe fest watȝ ilyche ful fiften dayes,

With alle þe mete & þe mirþe þat men couþe a-vyse;

Such glaumande gle glorious to here,

Dere dyn vp-on day, daunsyng on nyȝtes,

48   Al watȝ hap vpon heȝe in halleȝ & chambreȝ,

With lordeȝ & ladies, as leuest him þoȝt;

With all þe wele of þe worlde þay woned þer samen,

Þe most kyd knyȝteȝ vnder krystes seluen,

52   & þe louelokkest ladies þat euer lif haden,

& he þe comlokest kyng þat þe court haldes;

For al watȝ þis fayre folk in her first age,

on sille;

56   Þe hapnest vnder heuen,

Kyng hyȝest mon of wylle,

Hit were[1] now gret nye to neuen
So hardy a here on hille.

IV.

60　Wyle nw ȝer watȝ so ȝep þat hit watȝ nwe cummen,
　　þat day doubble on þe dece watȝ þe douth serued,
　　Fro þe kyng watȝ cummen with knyȝtes in to þe halle,
　　þe chauntre of þe chapel cheued to an ende ;
64　Loude crye watȝ þer kest of clerkeȝ & oþer,
　　Nowel nayted o-newe, neuened ful ofte ;
　　& syþen riche forth runnen to reche honde-selle,
　　Ȝeȝed ȝeres ȝiftes on hiȝ, ȝelde hem bi hond,
68　Debated busyly aboute þo giftes ;
　　Ladies laȝed ful loude, þoȝ þay lost haden,
　　& he þat wan watȝ not wroþe, þat may ȝe wel trawe.
　　Alle þis mirþe þay maden to þe mete tyme ;
72　When þay had waschen, worþyly þay wenten to sete,
　　þe best burne ay abof, as hit best semed ;
　　Whene Guenore ful gay, grayþed in þe myddes,
　　Dressed on þe dere des, dubbed al aboute,
76　Smal sendal bisides, a selure hir ouer
　　Of tryed Tolouse, of Tars tapites in-noghe,
　　þat were enbrawded & beten wyth þe best gemmes,
　　þat myȝt be preued of prys wyth penyes to bye,
80　　　　　　　　　in daye ;
　　　　þe comlokest to discrye,
　　　　þer glent with yȝen gray,
　　　　A semloker þat euer he syȝe,
84　　　　Soth moȝt no mon say.

V.

　　Bot Arthure wolde not ete til al were serued,
　　He watȝ so Ioly of his Ioyfnes, & sum-quat child gered,
　　His lif liked hym lyȝt, he louied þe lasse
88　Auþer to lenge lye, or to longe sitte,

1 werere, MS.

Marginal notes:

They celebrate the New Year with great joy.

[Fol. 92.]

Gifts are demanded and bestowed.

Lords and ladies take their seats at the table.

Queen Guenever appears gaily dressed.

A lady fairer of form might no one say he had ever before seen.

Arthur would not eat,

nor would he long sit

So bisied him his ʒonge blod & his brayn wylde;
& also anoþer maner meued him eke,
þat he þurʒ nobelay had nomen, he wolde neuer ete
92 Vpon such a dere day, er hym deuised were

until he had wit-
nessed a " won-
drous adventure"
of some kind.

Of sum auenturus þyng an vncouþe tale,
Of sum mayn meruayle, þat he myʒt trawe,
Of¹ alderes, of armes, of oþer auenturus,
96 Oþer sum segg hym bi-soʒt of sum siker knyʒt,
To Ioyne wyth hym in iustyng in Iopardé to lay,
Lede lif for lyf, leue vchon oþer,
As fortune wolde fulsun hom þe fayrer to haue.
100 þis watʒ [þe] kynges countenaunce where he in court
were,
At vch farand fest among his fre meny,
in halle;

He of face so
bold makes much
mirth with all.
[Fol. 92b.] 104

þer-fore of face so fere,
He stiʒtleʒ stif in stalle,
Ful ʒep in þat nw ʒere,
Muche mirthe he mas with alle.

VI.

The king talks
with his knights.

Thus þer stondes in stale þe stif kyng his-seluen,
108 Talkkande bifore þe hyʒe table of trifles ful hende;

Gawayne,

There gode Gawan watʒ grayþed, Gwenore bisyde,

Agravayn,

& Agrauayn a la dure mayn on þat oþer syde sittes,
Boþe þe kynges sister sunes, & ful siker kniʒtes;

Bishop Bawde-
wyn,
and Ywain sit
on the dais.

112 Bischop Bawdewyn abof bi-gineʒ þe table,
& Ywan, Vryn son, ette wit hymseluen;
þise were diʒt on þe des, & derworþly serued,
& siþen mony siker segge at þe sidbordeʒ.

The first course
is served with
cracking of trum-
pets.

116 þen þe first cors come with crakkyng of trumpes,
Wyth mony baner ful bryʒt, þat þer-bi henged,
Nwe nakryn noyse with þe noble pipes,
Wylde werbles & wyʒt wakned lote,
120 þat mony hert ful hiʒe hef at her towches;

¹ Of of, in MS.

Dayntes dryuen þer-wyth of ful dere metes,

Foysoun of þe fresche, & on so fele disches,

Þat pine to fynde þe place þe peple bi-forne ·

124 For to sette þe syluener,[1] þat sere sewes halden,

on clothe ;

Iche lede as he loued hym-selue

Þer laght with-outen loþe,

128 Ay two had disches twelue,

Good ber, & bryȝt wyn boþe.

It consisted of all dainties in season.

Each two had dishes twelve,

good beer and bright wine both.

VII.

Now wyl I of hor seruise say yow no more,

For vch wyȝe may wel wite no wont þat þer were ;

132 An oþer noyse ful newe neȝed biliue,

Þat þe lude myȝt haf leue liflode to cach.

For vneþe watȝ þe noyce not a whyle sesed,

& þe fyrst cource in þe court kyndely serued,

136 Þer hales in at þe halle dor an aghlich mayster,

On þe most on þe molde on mesure hyghe ;

Fro þe swyre to þe swange so sware & so þik,

& his lyndes & his lymes so longe & so grete,

140 Half etayn in erde I hope þat he were.

Bot mon most I algate mynn hym to bene,

& þat þe myriest in his muckel þat myȝt ride ;

For of bak & of brest al were his bodi sturne,

144 Bot his wombe & his wast were worthily smale,

& alle his fetures folȝande, in forme þat he hade,

ful clene ;

For wonder of his hwe men hade,

148 Set in his semblaunt sene ;

He ferde as freke were fade,

& ouer-al enker grene.

There was no want of anything.

Scarcely had the first course commenced,

when there rushes in at the hall-door a knight ;

the tallest on earth

[Fol. 93.]

he must have been.

His back and breast were great,

but his belly and waist were small.

VIII.

Ande al grayþed in grene þis gome & his wedes,

152 A strayt cote ful streȝt, þat stek on his sides,

He was clothed entirely in green

[1] sylueren (?) (dishes).

A mere mantile abof, mensked with-inne,
With pelure pured apert þe pane ful clene,
With blyþe blaunner ful bryȝt, & his hod boþe,
156 Þat watȝ laȝt fro his lokkeȝ, & layde on his schulderes;
Heme wel haled, hose of þat same grene,

His spurs were of bright gold.

Þat spenet on his sparlyr, & clene spures vnder,
Of bryȝt golde, vpon silk bordes, barred ful ryche,
160 & scholes vnder schankes, þere þe schalk rides;
& alle his vesture uerayly watȝ clene verdure,
Boþe þe barres of his belt & oþer blyþe stones,
Þat were richely rayled in his aray clene,

His saddle was embroidered with birds and flies.

164 Aboutte hym-self & his sadel, vpon silk werkeȝ,
Þat were to tor for to telle of tryfles þe halue,
Þat were enbrauded abof, wyth bryddes & flyȝes,
With gay gaudi of grene, þe golde ay in myddes;
168 Þe pendauntes of his payttrure, þe proude cropure,
His molaynes, & alle þe metail anamayld was þenue,
Þe steropes þat he stod on, stayned of þe same,
& his arsounȝ al after, & his aþel sturtes,
172 Þat euer glemered[1] & glent al of grene stones.

The foal that he rode upon was green;

Þe fole þat he ferkkes on, fyn of þat ilke,
    sertayn;
A grene hors gret & þikke,

it was a steed full stiff to guide.

176 A stede ful stif to strayne,
In brawden brydel quik,
To þe gome he watȝ ful gayn.

[Fol. 93a.]

IX.

Gaily was the knight attired.

Wel gay watȝ þis gome gered in grene,
180 & þe here of his hed of his hors swete;
Fayre fannand fax vmbe-foldes his schulderes;

His great beard, like a bush, hung on his breast.

A much berd as[2] a busk ouer his brest henges,
Þat wyth his hiȝlich here, þat of his hed reches,
184 Watȝ enesed al vmbe-torne, a-bof his elbowes,

[1] glemed (?).   [2] as as, in MS.

þat half his armes þer vnder were halched in þe wyse
Of a kyngeȝ capados, þat closes his swyre.
þe mane of þat mayn hors much to hit lyke,
188 Wel cresped & cemmed wyth knottes ful mony,
Folden in wyth fildore aboute þe fayre grene,
Ay a herle of þe here, an oþer of golde;
þe tayl & his toppyng twynnen of a sute,
192 & bounden boþe wyth a bande of a bryȝt grene,
Dubbed wyth ful dere stoneȝ, as þe dok lasted,
Syþen þrawen wyth a þwong a þwarle knot alofte,
þer mony belleȝ ful bryȝt of brende golde rungen.
196 Such a fole vpon folde, ne freke þat hym rydes,
Watȝ neuer sene in þat sale wyth syȝt er þat tyme,
with yȝe;
He loked as layt so lyȝt,
200 So sayd al þat hym syȝe,
Hit semed as no mon myȝt,
Vnder his dyntteȝ dryȝe.

X.

Wheþer hade he no helme ne hawb[e]rgh nauþer,
204 Ne no pysan, ne no plate þat pented to armes,
Ne no schafte, ne no schelde, to schwne ne to smyte,
Bot in his on honde he hade a holyn bobbe,
þat is grattest in grene, when greueȝ ar bare,
208 & an ax in his oþer, a hoge & vn-mete,
A spetos sparþe to expoun in spelle quo-so myȝt;
þe hede of an elnȝerde þe large lenkþe hade,
þe grayn al of grene stele and of golde hewen,
212 þe bit burnyst bryȝt, with a brod egge,
As wel schapen to schere as scharp rasores;
þe stele of a stif staf þe sturne hit bi-grypte,
þat watȝ waunden wyth yrn to þe wandeȝ ende,
216 & al bigrauen with grene, in gracons[1] werkes;

The horse's mane was decked with golden threads.

Its tail was bound with a green band.

Such a foal nor a knight were never before seen.

It seemed that no man might endure his dints.

The knight carried neither spear nor shield.

In one hand was a holly bough,

in the other an axe,

the edge of which was as keen as a sharp razor,

[Fol. 94.]
and the handle was encased in

[1] gracious (?).

iron, curiously "graven with green, in gracious works."
A lace lapped aboute, þat louked at þe hede,
& so after þe halme halched ful ofte,
Wyth tryed tasseleȝ þerto tacched in-noghee,

Thus arrayed the Green Knight enters the hall,
220 On botounȝ of þe bryȝt grene brayden ful ryche.
Þis haþel heldeȝ hym in, & þe halle entres,
Driuande to þe heȝe dece, dut he no woþe,

without saluting any one.
Haylsed he neuer one, bot heȝe he ouer loked.

224 Þe fyrst word þat he warp, "wher is," he sayd,

He asks for the "governor" of the company,
"Þe gouernour of þis gyng? gladly I wolde
Se þat segg in syȝt, & with hym self speke
    raysoun."

228   To knyȝteȝ he kest his yȝe,
    & reled hym vp & doun,

and looks for the most renowned.
    He stemmed & con studie,
    Quo walt þer most renoun.

XI.

Much they mar- vel to see a man and a horse
232 Ther watȝ lokyng on lenþe, þe lude to be-holde,
For vch mon had meruayle quat hit mene myȝt,
Þat a haþel & a horse myȝt such a hwe lach,

as green as grass.
As growe grene as þe gres & grener hit semed,
236 Þen grene aumayl on golde lowande bryȝter;
Al studied þat þer stod, & stalked hym nerre,

Never before had they seen such a sight as this.
Wyth al þe wonder of þe worlde, what he worch schulde
For fele sellyeȝ had þay sen, bot such neuer are,
240 For-þi for fantoum & fayryȝe þe folk þere hit demed;

They were afraid to answer,
Þerfore to answare watȝ arȝe mony aþel freke,
& al stouned at his steuen, & ston-stil seten,
In a swoghe sylence þurȝ þe sale riche

and were as silent as if sleep had taken pos- session of them;
244 As al were slypped vpon slepe so slaked hor loteȝ
    in hyȝe;
    I deme hit not al for doute,

some from fear and others from courtesy.
    Bot sum for cortaysye,
248   Bot let hym þat al schulde loute,
    Cast vnto þat wyȝe.

XII.

þenn Arþour bifore þe hiȝ dece þat auenture byholdeȝ, Arthur salutes the Green Knight,
& rekenly hym reuerenced, for rad was he neuer,

252 & sayde, " wyȝe, welcum iwys to þis place,
þe hede of þis ostel Arthour I hat; [Fol. 94b.] bids him welcome, and invites him to stay awhile.
Liȝt luflych adoun, & lenge, I þe praye,
& quat so þy wylle is, we schal wyt after."

256 "Nay, as help me," quoth þe haþel, "he þat on hyȝe syttes, The knight says that he will not tarry.
To wone any quyle in þis won, hit watȝ not myn ernde;
Bot for þe los of þe lede is lyft vp so hyȝe,
& þy burȝ & þy burnes best ar holden,

260 Stifest vnder stel-gere on stedes to ryde,
þe wyȝtest and þe worþyest of þe worldes kynde, He seeks the most valiant that he may prove him.
Preue for to play wyth in oþer pure laykeȝ;
& here is kydde cortaysye, as I haf herd carp,

264 & þat hatȝ wayned me hider, I-wyis, at þis tyme.
ȝe may be seker bi þis braunch þat I bere here,
þat I passe as in pes, & no plyȝt seche; He comes in peace.
For had I founded in fere, in feȝtyng wyse,

268 I haue a hauberghe at home & a helme boþe, At home, however, he has both shield and spear.
A schelde, & a scharp spere, schinande bryȝt,
Ande oþer weppenes to welde, I wene wel als,
Bot for I wolde no were, my wedeȝ ar softer.

272 Bot if þou be so bold as alle burneȝ tellen,
þou wyl grant me godly þe gomen þat I ask,
bi ryȝt."

Arthour con onsware, Arthur assures him that he shall not fail to find an opponent worthy of him.
276 & sayd, "syr cortays knyȝt,
If þou craue batayl bare,
Here fayleȝ þou not to fyȝt."

XIII.

" Nay, frayst I no fyȝt, in fayth I þe telle, " I seek no fight," says the knight.
280 Hit arn aboute on þis bench bot berdleȝ chylder; " 'Here are only beardless children.'
If I were hasped in armes on a heȝe stede, " Here is no man to match me.
Here is no mon me to mach, for myȝteȝ so wayke.

THE REQUEST OF THE GREEN KNIGHT.

For-þy I craue in þis court a crystemas gomen,

Here are brave ones many,
284 For hit is ȝol & nwe ȝer, & here ar ȝeþ mony;
If any so hardy in þis hous holdeȝ hym-seluen,

if any be bold enough to 'strike a stroke for another,'
Be so bolde in his blod, brayn in hys hede,
þat dar stifly strike a strok for an oþer,

288 I schal gif hym of my gyft þys giserne ryche,

this axe shall be his;
þis ax, þat is heué in-nogh, to hondele as hym lykes,

[Fol. 95.]
& I schal bide þe fyrst bur, as bare as I sitte.
If any freke be so felle to fonde þat I telle,

292 Lepe lyȝtly me to, & lach þis weppen,
I quit clayme hit for euer, kepe hit as his auen,

but I shall give him a 'stroke' in return
& I schal stonde hym a strok, stif on þis flet,
Elleȝ þou wyl diȝt me þe dom to dele hym an oþer,

296   barlay;
& ȝet gif hym respite,

within a twelve-month and a day."
A twelmonyth & a day;
Now hyȝe, & let se tite

300 Dar any her-inne oȝt say."

XIV.

Fear kept all silent.
If he hem stowned vpon fyrst, stiller were þanne
Alle þe hered-men in halle, þe hyȝ & þe loȝe;

The knight rolled his red eyes about,
þe renk on his rounce hym ruched in his sadel,
304 & runisch-ly his rede yȝen he reled aboute,

and bent his bristly green brows.
Bende his bresed broȝeȝ, bly-cande grene,

Waving his beard awhile, he exclaimed:
Wayued his berde for to wayte quo-so wolde ryse.
When non wolde kepe hym with carp he coȝed ful hyȝe,

308 Ande rimed hym ful richley, & ryȝt hym to speke:

"What! is this 'Arthur's court?
"What, is þis Arþures hous," quoth þe haþel þenne,
"þat al þe rous rennes of, þurȝ ryalmes so mony?
Where is now your sourquydrye & your conquestes,

312 Your gryndel-layk, & your greme, & your grete wordes?

Forsooth the renown of the Round Table is overturned 'with a word of one man's speech."
Now is þe reuel & þe renoun of þe rounde table
Ouer-walt wyth a worde of on wyȝes speche;
For al dares for drede, withoute dynt schewed!"

316 Wyth þis he laȝes so loude, þat þe lorde greued;

þe blod schot for scham in-to his schyre face
    & lere;
He wex as wroth as wynde,
320   So did alle þat þer were,
þe kyng as kene bi kynde,
þen stod þat stif mon nere.

Arthur blushes for shame.

He waxes as wroth as the wind.

XV.

Ande sayde, " haþel, by heuen þyn askyng is nys,
324 & as þou foly hatȝ frayst, fynde þe be-houes;
I know no gome þat is gast of þy grete wordes.
Gif me now þy geserne, vpon godeȝ halue,
    & I schal bayþen þy bone, þat þou boden habbes."
328 Lyȝtly lepeȝ he hym to, & laȝt at his honde;
þen feersly þat oþer freke vpon fote lyȝtis.
Now hatȝ Arthure his axe, & þe halme grypeȝ,
    & sturnely stureȝ hit aboute, þat stryke wyth hit þoȝt.
332 þe stif mon hym bifore stod vpon hyȝt,
Herre þen ani in þe hous by þe hede & more;
Wyth sturne schere[1] þer he stod, he stroked his berde,
    & wyth a countenaunçe dryȝe he droȝ doun his cote,
336 No more mate ne dismayd for hys mayn dinteȝ,
þen any burne vpon bench hade broȝt hym to drynk
    of wyne,
Gawan, þat sate bi þe quene,
340   To þe kyng he can enclyne,
" I be-seche now with saȝeȝ sene,
þis melly mot be myne."

He assures the knight that no one is afraid of his great words.

[Fol. 95b.]

Arthur seizes his axe.

The knight, stroking his beard, awaits the blow, and with a "dry countenance" draws down his coat.

Sir Gawayne beseeches the king to let him undertake the blow.

XVI.

" Wolde ȝe, worþilych lorde," quoth Gawan to þe kyng,
344 " Bid me boȝe fro þis benche, & stonde by yow þere,
þat I wyth-oute vylanye myȝt voyde þis table,
    & þat my legge lady lyked not ille,

He asks permission to leave the table; he says,

[1] ohere (?).

I wolde com to your counseyl, bifore your cort ryche.

348 For me þink hit not semly, as hit is soþ knawen,

þer such an askyng is heuened so hyȝe in your sale,

þaȝ ȝe ȝour-self be talenttyf to take hit to your-seluen,

Whil mony so bolde yow aboute vpon bench sytten,

352 þat vnder heuen, I hope, non haȝer er of wylle,

No better bodyes on bent, þer baret is rered;

I am þe wakkest, I wot, and of wyt feblest,

& lest lur of my lyf, quo laytes þe soþe,

356 Bot for as much as ȝe ar myn em, I am only to prayse,

No bounté bot your blod I in my bodé knowe;

& syþen þis note is so nys, þat noȝt hit yow falles,

& I haue frayned hit at yow fyrst, foldeȝ hit to me,

360 & if I carp not comlyly, let alle þis cort rych,

bout blame."

Ryche to-geder con roun,

& syþen þay redden alle same,

364 To ryd þe kyng wyth croun,

& gif Gawan þe game.

XVII.

Þen comaunded þe kyng þe knyȝt for to ryse;

& he ful radly vp ros, & ruchched hym fayre,

368 Kneled doun bifore þe kyng, & cacheȝ þat weppen;

& he luflyly hit hym laft, & lyfte vp his honde,

& gef hym goddeȝ blessyng, & gladly hym biddes

þat his hert & his honde schulde hardi be boþe.

372 "Kepe þe cosyn," quoth þe kyng, "þat þou on kyrf sette,

& if þou redeȝ hym ryȝt, redly I trowe,

þat þou schal byden þe bur þat he schal bede after."

Gawan gotȝ to þe gome, with giserne in honde,

376 & he baldly hym bydeȝ, he bayst neuer þe helder.

Þen carppeȝ to syr Gawan þe knyȝt in þe grene,

"Refourme we oure forwardes, er we fyrre passe.

Fyrst I eþe þe, haþel, how þat þou hattes,

380 þat þou me telle truly, as I tryst may ?"
   "In god fayth," quoth þe goode knyȝt, "Gawan I hatte,

   þat bede- þe þis buffet, quat-so bi-falleȝ after,
   & at þis tyme twelmonyth take at þe anoþer,
384 Wyth what weppen so þou wylt, & wyth no wyȝ elleȝ,
                                    on lyue."
          þat oþer onswareȝ agayn,
          "Sir Gawan, so mot I þryue,.
388   As I am ferly fayn,

          þis dint þat þou schal dryue."

XVIII.

   "Bi gog," quoth þe grene knyȝt, "syr Gawan, me lykes,

   þat I schal fange at þy fust þat I haf frayst here ;
392 & þou hatȝ redily rehersed, bi resoun ful trwe,

   Clanly al þe couenaunt þat I þe kynge asked,
   Saf þat þou schal siker me, segge, by þi trawþe,

   þat þou schal seche me þi-self, where-so þou hopes
396 I may be funde vpon folde, & foch þe such wages
   As þou deles me to day, bifore þis douþe ryche."

   "Where schulde I wale þe," quoth Gauan, "where is

          þy place ?
   I wot neuer where þou wonyes, bi hym þat me wroȝt,
400 Ne I know not þe, knyȝt, þy cort, ne þi name.
   Bot teche me truly þer-to, & telle me howe þou hattes,

   & I schal ware alle my wyt to wynne me þeder,
   & þat I swere þe for soþe, & by my seker traweþ."

404 "þat is in-nogh in nwe ȝer, hit nedes no more,"
   Quoth þe gome in þe grene to Gawan þe hende,
   "Gif I þe telle trwly, quen I þe tape haue,

   & þou me smoþely hatȝ smyten, smartly I þe teche
408 Of my hous, & my home, & myn owen nome,
   þen may þou frayst my fare, & forwardeȝ holde,
   & if I spende no speche, þenne spedeȝ þou þe better,

   For þou may leng in þy londe, & layt no fyrre,
412   bot slokes ,

Take now thy grim tool, and let us see how thou knockest."

> Ta now þy grymme tole to þe,
> & let se how þou enokeȝ."
> "Gladly syr, for soþe,"
> 416   Quoth Gawan; his ax he strokes.

XIX.

The Green Knight

> The grene knyȝt vpon grounde grayþely hym dresses,
> A littel lut wiþ þe hede, þe lere he diskouereȝ,

puts his long lovely locks aside and lays bare his neck.

> His longe louelych lokkeȝ he layd ouer his croun,
> 420 Let þe naked nec to þe note schewe.
> Gauan gripped to his ax, & gederes hit on hyȝt,
> þe kay fote on þe folde he be-fore sette,

Sir Gawayne lets fall his axe,

> Let hit doun lyȝtly lyȝt on þe naked,
> 424 þat þe scharp of þe schalk schyndered þe bones,

and severs the head from the body.

> & schrank þurȝ þe schyire grece, & scade hit in twynne,
> þat þe bit of þe broun stel bot on þe grounde.

The head falls to the earth. Many kick it aside with their feet.

> þe fayre hede fro þe halce hit [felle] to þe erþe,
> 428 þat fele hit foyned wyth her fete, þere hit forth roled;
> þe blod brayd fro þe body, þat blykked on þe grene;

The knight never falters;

> & nawþer faltered ne fel þe freke neuer-þe-helder,
> Bot styþly he start forth vpon styf schonkes,

he rushes forth, seizes his head,

> 432 & ru[n]yschly he raȝt out, þere as renkkeȝ stoden,
> Laȝt to his lufly hed, & lyft hit vp sone;
> & syþen boȝeȝ to his blonk, þe brydel he cachcheȝ,

steps into the saddle,

> Steppeȝ in to stel bawe & strydeȝ alofte,

holding the while the head in his hand by the hair,

> 436 & his hede by þe here in his honde haldeȝ;
> & as sadly þe segge hym in his sadel sette,
> As non vnhap had hym ayled, þaȝ hedleȝ ho we,[1]
>   in stedde;

and turns his horse about.

[Fol. 97.]

> 440   He brayde his bluk[2] aboute,
>   þat vgly bodi þat bledde,
>   Moni on of hym had doute,
>   Bi þat his resounȝ were redde.

---

[1] he were (?) or nowe (?).   [2] blunk (?).

XX.

444 For þe hede in his honde he halde; vp euen,
   To-ward þe derrest on þe dece he dresse; þe face,
   & hit lyfte vp þe y;e-lydde;, & loked ful brode,
   & meled þus much with his muthe, as ;e may now here.
448 "Loke, Gawan, þou be grayþe to go as þou hette;,
   & layte as lelly til þou me, lude, fynde,
   As þou hat; hette in þis halle, herande þise kny;tes;
   To þe grene chapel þou chose, I charge þe to fotte,
452 Such a dunt as þou hat; dalt disserued þou habbe;,
   To be ;ederly ;olden on nw ;eres morn;
   þe kny;t of þe grene chapel men knowen me mony;
   For-þi me for to fynde if þou frayste;, fayle; þou neuer,
456 þer-fore com, oþer recreaunt be calde þe be-houes."
   With a runisch rout þe rayne; he terne;,
   Halled out at þe hal-dor, his hed in his hande,
   þat þe fyr of þe flynt fla;e fro fole houes.
460 To quat kyth he be-com, kn[e]we non þere,
   Neuer more þen þay wyste fram queþen he wat; wonnen;
        what þenne?
      þe kyng & Gawen þare,
464   At þat grene þay la;e & grenne,
      ;et breued wat; hit ful bare,
      A meruayl among þo menne.

XXI.

   þa; Arþer þe hende kyng at hert hade wonder,
468 He let no semblaunt be sene, bot sayde ful hy;e
   To þe comlych quene, wyth cortays speche,
   "Dere dame, to day demay yow neuer;
   Wel by-commes such craft vpon cristmasse,
472 Laykyng of enterlude;, to la;e & to syng.
   Among þise, kynde caroles of kny;te; & ladye;;
   Neuer-þe-lece to my mete I may me wel dres,
   For I haf sen a selly, I may not for-sake."
476 He glent vpon syr Gawen, & gaynly he sayde,

The head lifts up its eyelids,

and addresses Sir Gawayne; "Look thou, be ready to go as thou hast promised,

and seek till thou findest me.

Get thee to the Green Chapel,

there to receive a blow on New Year's morn.

Fail thou never;

Come, or recreant be called."

The Green Knight then rushes out of the hall, his head in his hand.

At that green one Arthur and Gawayne "laugh and grin."

Arthur addresses the queen:

"Dear dame, be not dismayed; such marvels well become the Christmas festival;

I may now go to meat.

:" Now syr, heng vp þyn ax, þat hatȝ in-nogh hewen."
& hit watȝ don abof þe dece, on doser to henge,
þer alle men for meruayl myȝt on hit loke,
480 & bi trwe tytel þer-of to telle þe wonder.

þenne þay boȝed to a borde þise burnes to-geder,
þe kyng & þe gode knyȝt, & kene men hem serued
Of alle dayntyeȝ double, as derrest myȝt falle,
484 Wyth alle maner of mete & mynstralcie boþe ;
Wyth wele walt þay þat day, til worþed an ende,
in londe.

Now þenk wel, syr Gawan,
488 For woþe þat þou ne wonde,
þis auenture forto frayn,
þat þou hatȝ tan ou honde.

[FYTTE THE SECOND.]

I.

THIS hanselle hatȝ Arthur of auenturus on fyrst,
492   In ȝonge ȝer, for he ȝerned ȝelpyng to here,
Thaȝ hym wordeȝ were wane, when þay to sete wenten ;
Now ar þay stoken of sturne werk staf-ful her hond.
Gawan watȝ glad to be-gynne þose gomneȝ in halle,
496 Bot þaȝ þe ende be heuy, haf ȝe no wonder ;
For þaȝ man ben mery in mynde, quen þay han mayn drynk,

A ȝere ȝernes ful ȝerne, & ȝeldeȝ neuer lyke,
þe forme to be fyniment foldeȝ ful selden.
500 For-þi þis ȝol ouer-ȝede, & þe ȝere after,
& vche sesoun serlepes sued after oþer ;

After crysten-masse com þe crabbed lentoun,
þat fr256 flesch wyth þe fysche & fode more symple ;
504 Bot þenne þe weder of þe worlde wyth wynter hit þrepeȝ,

Colde clengeȝ adoun, cloudeȝ vp-lyften,
Schyre schedeȝ þe rayn in schowreȝ ful warme,

Falleȝ vpon fayre flat, flowreȝ þere schewen,
508 Boþe groundeȝ & þe greueȝ grene ar her wedeȝ,
Bryddeȝ busken to bylde, & bremlych syngen,
For solace of þe softe somer þat sues þer-after,
    bi bonk ;
512   & blossumeȝ bolne to blowe,
   Bi raweȝ rych & ronk,
   þen noteȝ noble in-noȝe,
   Ar herde in wod so wlonk.

The groves become green; Birds build and sing, for joy of the summer that follows;

Blossoms begin to bloom,

and noble notes are heard in the woods.
[Fol. 98.]

II.

516 After þe sesoun of somer wyth þe soft wyndeȝ,
Quen ȝeferus syfleȝ hym-self on sedeȝ & erbeȝ,
Wela-wynne is þe wort þat woxes þer-oute,
When þe donkande dewe dropeȝ of þe leueȝ,
520 To bide a blysful blusch of þe briȝt sunne.
Bot þen hyȝes heruest, & hardenes hym sone,
Warneȝ hym for þe wynter to wax ful rype ;
He dryues wyth droȝt þe dust for to ryse,
524 Fro þe face of the folde to flyȝe ful hyȝe ;
Wroþe wynde of þe welkyn wrasteleȝ with þe sunne,
þe leueȝ lancen fro þe lynde, & lyȝten on þe grounde,
& al grayes þe gres, þat grene watȝ ere ;
528 þenne al rypeȝ & roteȝ þat ros vpon fyrst,
& þus ȝirneȝ þe ȝere in ȝisterdayeȝ mony,
& wynter wyndeȝ aȝayn, as þe worlde askeȝ
    no sage.
532   Til meȝel-mas mone,
   Watȝ cumen wyth wynter wage ;
   þen þenkkeȝ Gawan ful sone,
   Of his anious uyage.

After the soft winds of summer,

beautiful are the flowers wet with dew drops.

But harvest approaches soon,

and drives the dust about.

The leaves drop off the trees, the grass becomes gray, and all ripens and rots.

Winter winds round again,

and then Sir Gawayne thinks of his dread journey.

III.

536 ȝet quyl al-hal-day with Arþer he lenges,
& he made a fare on þat fest, for þe frekeȝ sake,
With much reuel & ryche of þe rounde table ;

On All-hallows day Arthur makes a feast for his nephew's sake.

2

Kny₃te₃ ful cortays & comlych ladies,

540 Al for luf of þat lede in longynge þay were,

Bot neuer-þe-iece ne þe later þay neuened bot merþe,

Mony ioyle₃ for þat ientyle iape₃ þer maden.

After meat, Sir Gawayne thus speaks to his uncle :

For aftter mete, with mournyng he mele₃ to his eme,

544 & speke₃ of his passage, & pertly he sayde,

"Now, liege lord, I ask leave of you,

"Now, lege lorde of my lyf, leue I yow ask;

₃e knowe þe cost of þis cace, kepe I no more

To telle yow tene₃ þer-of neuer bot trifel ;

for I am bound on the morn to seek the Green Knight."

548 Bot I am boun to þe bur barely to-morne,

To sech þe gome of þe grene, as god wyl me wysse."

Þenne þe best of þe bur₃ bo₃ed to-geder,

Aywan, & Errik, & oþer ful mony,

[Fol. 98b.] 552 Syr Doddinaual de Sauage, þe duk of Clarence,

Launcelot, & Lyonel, & Lucan þe gode,

Syr Boos, & sir Byduer, big men boþe,

Many nobles, the best of the court, counsel and comfort him.

& mony oþer menskful, with Mador de la Port.

556 Alle þis companyy of court com þe kyng nerre,

For to counseyl þe kny₃t, with care at her hert ;

Much sorrow prevails in the hall.

Þere wat₃ much derue[1] doel driuen in þe sale,

Þat so worthe as Wawan schulde wende on þat ernde,

560 To dry₃e a delful dynt, & dele no more

wyth bronde.

Þe kny₃t mad ay god chere,

& sayde, "quat schuld I wonde,

Gawayne declares that he has nothing to fear.

564 Of destines derf & dere,

What may mon do bot fonde ?"

IV.

On the morn he asks for his arms.

He dowelle₃ þer al þat day, and dresse₃ on þe morn,

Aske₃ erly hys arme₃, & alle were þay bro₃t

A carpet is spread on the floor,

568 Fyrst a tule tapit, ty₃t ouer þe flet,

& miche wat₃ þe gyld gere þat ₃lent þer alofte ;

and he steps thereon.

Þe stif mon steppe₃ þeron, & þe stel hondele₃;

[1] derne (?).

Dubbed in a dublet of a dere tars,

572 & syþen a crafty capados, closed aloft,
þat wyth a bryȝt blaunner was bounden with-inne;
Þenne set þay þe sabatounȝ vpon þe segge foteȝ,
His legeȝ lapped in stel with luflych greueȝ,

576 With polayneȝ piched þer-to, policed ful clene,
Aboute his kneȝ knaged wyth knoteȝ of golde;
Queme quyssewes þen, þat coyntlych closed
His thik þrawen þyȝeȝ, with þwonges to tachched;

580 & syþen þe brawden bryne of bryȝt stel ryngeȝ,
Vmbe-weued þat wyȝ, vpon wlonk stuffe;
& wel bornyst brace vpon his boþe armes,
With gode cowters & gay, & gloueȝ of plate,

584 & alle þe godlych gere þat hym gayn schulde
þat tyde;
Wyth ryche cote armure,
His gold sporeȝ spend with pryde,

588 Gurde wyth a bront ful sure,
With silk sayn vmbe his syde.

[Fol. 99a.]

He is dubbed in a doublet of Tarsic silk, and a well made hood.

They set steel shoes on his feet, and lap his legs in steel greaves.

Fair cuisses enclose his thighs,

and afterwards they put on the steel habergeon,

well-burnished braces, elbow pieces, and gloves of plate.

Over all this is placed the coat armour. His spurs are then fixed, and his sword is attached to his side by a silken girdle.

V.

When he watȝ hasped in armes, his harnays watȝ ryche,
þe lest lachet ou[þ]er loupe lemed of golde;

592 So harnayst as he watȝ he herkneȝ his masse,
Offred & honoured at þe heȝe auter;
Syþen he comeȝ to þe kyng & to his cort fereȝ,
Lacheȝ lufly his leue at lordeȝ & ladyeȝ;

596 & þay hym kyst & conueyed, bikende hym to kryst.
Bi þat watȝ Gryngolet grayth, & gurde with a sadel,
þat glemed ful gayly with mony golde frenges,
Ay quere naylet ful nwe for þat note ryched;

600 þe brydel barred a-boute, with bryȝt golde bounden,
þe apparayl of þe payttrure, & of þe proude skyrteȝ,
þe cropore, & þe couertor, acorded wyth þe arsouneȝ;
& al watȝ rayled on red ryche golde nayleȝ,

604 þat al glytered & glent as glem of þe sunne.

Thus arrayed the knight hears mass,

and afterwards takes leave of Arthur and his court.

By that time his horse Gringolet was ready,

the harness of which glittered like the "gleam of the sun."

Then Sir Ga-
wayne sets his
helmet upon his
head,

fastened behind
with a "uri-
soun,"

richly embroi-
dered with gems.

Þenne hentes he þe helme, & hastily hit kysses,

Þat watȝ stapled stifly, & stoffed wyth-inne ;

Hit watȝ hyȝe on his hede, hasped bihynde,

608 Wyth a lyȝt lyn vrysoun ouer þe auentayle,

Enbrawden & bounden wyth þe best gemmeȝ,

On brode sylkyn borde, & bryddeȝ on semeȝ,

As papiayeȝ paynted pernyng bitwene,

612 Tortors & trulofeȝ entayled so þyk,

As mony burde þer-aboute had ben seuen wynter
in toune ;

The circle around
the helmet was
decked with dia-
monds.

616 Þe cercle watȝ more o prys,

Þat vmbe-clypped hys croun,

Of diamaunteȝ a deuys,

Þat boþe were bryȝt & broun.

VI.

Then they show
him his shield
with the "pent-
angle" of pure
gold.

Then þay schewed hym þe schelde, þat was of schyr gouleȝ,

620 Wyth þe pentangel de-paynt of pure golde hweȝ ;

He braydeȝ hit by þe baude-ryk, a-boute þe hals kestes,

Þat bisemed þe segge semlyly fayre.

The "pentangle"
was devised by
Solomon as a
token of truth.

& quy þe pentangel apendeȝ to þat prynce noble,

624 I am in tent yow to tellé, þof tary hyt me schulde ;

Hit is a syngne þat Salamon set sum-quyle,

In bytoknyng of trawþe, bi tytle þat hit habbeȝ,

[Fol. 99b.]

For hit is a figure þat haldeȝ fyue poynteȝ,

628 & vche lyne vmbe-lappeȝ & loukeȝ in oþer,

It is called the
endless knot.

& ay quere hit is eindeleȝ,[1] & Englych hit callen

Ouer-al, as I here, þe endeles knot.

For-þy hit acordeȝ to þis knyȝt, & to his cler armeȝ,

632 For ay faythful in fyue & sere fyue syþeȝ,

It well becomes
the good Sir Ga-
wayne,

Gawan watȝ for gode knawen, & as golde pured,

Voyded of vche vylany, wyth vertueȝ ennourned
in mote ;

636 For-þy þe pentangel nwe

He ber in schelde & cote,

1 emdeleȝ (?).

As tulk of tale most trwe,
& gentylest kny3t of lote.

a knight the truest of speech and the fairest of form.

VII.

640 Fyrst he wat3 funden fautle3 in his fyue wytte3,.
   & efte fayled neuer þe freke in his fyue fyngres,
   & alle his afyaunce vpon folde wat3 in þe fyue wounde3
   þat cryst ka3t on þe croys, as þe crede telle3;
644 & quere-so-euer þys mon in melly wat3 stad,
   His þro po3t wat3 in þat, þur3 alle oþer þynge3,
   þat alle his forsnes he fong at þe fyue ioye3,
   þat þe hende heuen quene had of hir chylde;
648 At þis cause þe kny3t comlyche hade
   In þe more half of his schelde hir ymage depaynted,
   þat quen he blusched þerto, his belde neuer payred.
   þe fyrst[1] fyue þat I finde þat þe frek vsed,
652 Wat3 fraunchyse, & fela3schyp for-be[2] al þyng;
   His clannes & his cortaysye croked were neuer,
   & pite, þat passe3 alle poynte3, þyse pure fyue
   Were harder happed on þat haþel þen on any oþer.
656 Now alle þese fyue syþe3, forsoþe, were fetled on þis kny3t,
   & vchone halched in oþer, þat non ende hade,
   & fyched vpon fyue poynte3, þat fayld neuer,
   Ne samned neuer in no syde, ne sundred nouþer,
660 With-outen ende at any noke [a]i quere fynde,
   Where-euer þe gomen bygan, or glod to an ende.
   þer-fore on his schene schelde schapen wat3 þe knot,
   þus alle wyth red golde vpon rede gowle3,
664 þat is þe pure pentaungel wyth þe peple called,
      with lore.
   Now grayþed is Gawan gay,
   & la3t his launce ry3t þore,
668 & gef hem alle goud day,
   He wende for euer more.

He was found faultless in his five wits.

His trust was in the five wounds.

The image of the Virgin was depicted upon his shield.

In cleanness and courtesy he was never found wanting,

therefore was the endless knot fastened on his shield.

[Fol. 100.]

Sir Gawayne seizes his lance and bids all "good day."

[1] fyft, in MS.   [2] for-bi (?).

VIII.

He spurs his horse and goes on his way.

He sperred þe sted wiþ þe spureȝ, & sprong on his way,

So stif þat þe ston fyr stroke out þer-after;

All that saw that seemly one mourned in their hearts.

672 Al þat seȝ þat semly syked in hert,

     & sayde soþly al same segges til oþer,

     Carande for þat comly, " bi kryst, hit is scaþe,

     þat þou, leude, schal be lost, þat art of lyf noble!

They declared that his equal was not to be found upon earth.

676 To fynde hys fere vpon folde, in fayth is not eþe;

     Warloker to haf wroȝt had more wyt bene,

     & haf dyȝt ȝonder dere a duk to haue worþed;

It would have been better for him to have been a leader of men,

     A lowande leder of ledeȝ in londe hym wel semeȝ,

680 & so had better haf ben þen britned to noȝt,

than to die by the hands of " an elvish man."

     Hadet wyth an aluisch mon, for angardeȝ pryde.

     Who knew euer any kyng such counsel to take,

     As knyȝteȝ in cauelounȝ on cryst-masse gomneȝ!"

Much was the warm water that poured from eyes that day.

684 Wel much watȝ þe warme water þat waltered of yȝen,

     When þat semly syre soȝt fro þo woneȝ

            þat[1] daye;

         He made non abode,

688   Bot wyȝtly went hys way,

Meanwhile many a weary way goes Sir Gawayne.

         Mony wylsum way he rode,

         þe bok as I herde say.

IX.

Now rides the knight through the realms of England.

Now rideȝ þis renk þurȝ þe ryalme of Logres,

692 Syr Gauan on godeȝ halue, þaȝ hym no gomen þoȝt;

     Oft, leudleȝ alone, he lengeȝ on nyȝteȝ,

     þer he fonde noȝt hym byfore þe fare þat he lyked;

He has no companion but his horse.

     Hade he no fere bot his fole, bi frytheȝ & douneȝ,

No men does he see till he approaches North Wales.

696 Ne no gome bot god, bi gate wyth to karp,

     Til þat he neȝed ful noghe[2] in to þe Norþe Waleȝ;

     Alle þe iles of Anglesay on lyft half he haldeȝ,

     & fareȝ ouer þe fordeȝ by þe for-londeȝ,

---

         [1] þad, in MS.   [2] nyghe (?).

700   Ouer at þe Holy-Hede, til he hade eft bonk

From Holyhead
he passes into
Wirral.

    In þe wyldrenesse of Wyrale ; wonde þer bot lyte

    Þat auþer god oþer gome wyth goud hert louied.·

[Fol. 100b.]
There he finds
but few that loved
God or man.

    & ay he frayned, as he ferde, at frekez þat he met,

704   If þay hade herde any karp of a knyȝt grene,

He enquires after
the Green Knight
of the Green
Chapel,

    In any grounde þer-aboute, of þe grene chapel ;[1]

    & al nykked hym wyth nay, þat neuer in her lyue

but can gain no
tidings of him.

    Þay seȝe neuer no segge þat watz of suche hwez

708   of grene.

      Þe knyȝt tok gates straunge,

      In mony a bonk vnbene,

His cheer oft
changed before
he found the
Chapel.

      His cher ful oft con chaunge,

712   Þat chapel er he myȝt sene.

X.

    Mony klyf he ouer-clambe in contrayez straunge,

Many a cliff he
climbed over ;

    Fer floten fro his frendez fremedly he rydez ;

    At vche warþe oþer water þer þe wyȝe passed,

Many a ford and
stream he cross-
ed, and every-
where he found a
foe.

716   He fonde a foo hym byfore, bot ferly hit were,

    & þat so foule & so felle, þat feȝt hym by-hode ;

    So mony meruayl bi mount þer þe mon fyndez,

It were too tedi-
ous to tell the
tenth part of his
adventures,

    Hit were to tore for to telle of þe tenþe dole.

720   Sumwhyle wyth wormez he werrez, & with wolues als,

with serpents,
wolves, and wild
men ;

    Sumwhyle wyth wodwos, þat woned in þe knarrez,

    Boþe wyth bullez & berez, & borez oþer-quyle,

with bulls, bears,
and boars.

    & etaynez, þat hym a-nelede, of þe heȝe felle ;

724   Nade he ben duȝty & dryȝe, & dryȝtyn had serued,

Had he not been
both brave and
good, doubtless
he had been dead.

    Douteles he hade ben ded, & dreped ful ofte.

    For werre wrathed hym not so much, þat wynter was

The sharp winter
was far worse
than any war that
ever troubled
him.

        wors,

    When þe colde cler water fro þe cloudez schadden,

728   & fres er hit falle myȝt to þe fale erþe ;

    Ner slayn wyth þe slete he sleped in his yrnes,

    Mo nyȝtez þen in-noghe in naked rokkez,

[1] clapel, in MS.

Þer as claterande fro þe crest þe colde borne renneȝ,

732   & henged heȝe ouer his hede in hard ẏsse-ikkles.

Thus in peril he
travels till Christ-
mas-eve.

Þus in peryl, & payne, & plytes ful harde,

Bi contray caryeȝ þis knyȝt, tyl kryst-masse euen,

al one;

736   Þe knyȝt wel þat tyde,

To the Virgin
Mary he prays to
guide him to
some abode.

To Mary made his mone,

Þat ho hym red to ryde,

[Fol. 101.]

& wysse hym to sum wone.

XI.

On the morn Sir
Gawayne finds
himself in a deep
forest,

740   Bi a mounte on þe morne meryly he rydes,

Into a forest ful dep, þat ferly watȝ wylde,

Hiȝe hilleȝ on vche a halue, & holt wodeȝ vnder,

where were old
oaks many a
hundred.

Of hore okeȝ ful hoge a hundreth to-geder;

744   Þe hasel & þe haȝ-þorne were harled al samen,

With roȝe raged mosse rayled ay-where,

Many sad birds
upon bare twigs
piped piteously
for the cold.

With mony bryddeȝ vnblyþe vpon bare twyges,

Þat pitosly þer piped fon pyne of þe colde.

748   Þe gome vpon Gryngolet glydeȝ hem vnder,

Through many a
mire he goes, that
he may celebrate
the birth of
Christ.

Þurȝ mony misy & myre, mon al hym one,

Carande for his costes, lest he ne keuer schulde,

To se þe seruy[1] of þat syre, þat on þat self nyȝt

752   Of a burde watȝ borne, oure baret to quelle;

He beseeches the
Virgin Mary to
direct him to
some lodging
where he may
hear mass.

& þerfore sykyng he sayde, "I be-seche þe, lorde,

& Mary, þat is myldest moder so dere,

Of sum herber, þer heȝly I myȝt here masse.

756   Ande þy matyneȝ to-morne, mekely I ask,

& þer-to prestly I pray my pater & aue,

& crede."

He rode in his prayere,

760   & cryed for his mysdede,

Blessing himself,
he says, "Cross
of Christ, speed
me!"

He sayned hym in syþes sere,

& sayde "cros kryst me spede!"

---

[1] seruyce (?).

XII.

Nade he sayned hym-self, segge, bot þrye,

764 Er he watʒ war iɴ þe wod of a won iɴ a mote.

Abof a lauɴde, on a lawe, loken vnder boʒeʒ,

Of mony borelych bole, aboute bi þe diches;

A castel þe comlokest þat euer knyʒt aʒte,

768 Pyched on a prayere, a park al aboute,

With a pyked palays, pyned ful þik,

þat vmbe-teʒe mony tre mo þeɴ two myle.

þat holde on þat on syde þe haþel auysed,

772 As hit schemered & schon þurʒ þe schyre okeʒ;

þenne hatʒ he hendly of his helme, & heʒly he þonkeʒ

Jesus & say[nt] Gilyan, þat gentyle ar boþe,

þat cortaysly hade hym kydde, & his cry herkened.

776 "Now bone hostel," coþe þe burne, "I be-seche yow ʒette!"

þenne gedereʒ he to Gryngolet with þe gilt heleʒ,

& he ful chauɴcely hatʒ chosen to þe chef gate,

þat broʒt bremly þe burne to þe bryge ende,

780   iɴ haste;

þe bryge watʒ breme vp-brayde,

þe ʒateʒ wer stoken faste,

þe walleʒ were wel arayed,

784   Hit dut no wyndeʒ blaste.

Scarcely had he blessed himself thrice,

when he saw a dwelling in the wood, set on a hill,

the comeliest castle he had ever beheld.

It shone as the sun through the bright oaks.

[Fol. 101b.]

Sir Gawayne goes to the chief gate,

and finds the draw-bridge raised, and the gates shut fast.

XIII.

þe burne bode on bonk, þat on blonk houed,

Of þe depe double dich þat drof to þe place,

þe walle wod iɴ þe water wonderly depe,

788 Ande eft a ful huge heʒt hit haled vpon lofte,

Of harde hewen ston vp to þe tableʒ,

Enbaned vnder þe abataylmeɴt, iɴ þe best lawe;

& syþen garyteʒ ful gaye gered bi-twene,

792 Wyth mony luflych loupe, þat louked ful clene;

A better barbican þat burne blusched vpon neuer;

& iɴnermore he be-helde þat halle ful hyʒe,

The knight abides on the bank,

and observes the "huge height,"

with its battlements and watch towers.

Bright and long were its round towers,
Towre telded bytwene trochet ful þik,

796 Fayre fylyolez þat fyzed, & ferlyly long,

with their well-made capitals.
With coruon coprounes, craftyly sleze ;

Chalk whyt chymnees þer ches he in-noze,

Vpon bastel rouez, þat blenked ful quyte ;

800 So mony pynakle payntet watz poudred ay quere,

Among þe castel carnelez, clambred so þik,

þat pared out of papure purely hit semed.

He thinks it fair enough if he might only come within the cloister.
þe fre freke on þe fole hit fayr in-n[o]ghe þozt,

804 If he myzt keuer to com þe cloyster wyth-inne,

To herber in þat hostel, whyl halyday lested
       auinant ;

He calls, and soon there comes a porter to know the knight's errand.
He calde, & sone þer com

808 A porter pure plesaunt,

On þo wal his ernd he nome,

& haylsed þe knyzt erraunt.

XIV.

"Good sir," says Gawayne, "ask the high lord of this house to grant me a lodging."
"Gode syr," quoth Gawan, "woldez þou go myn ernde,

812 To þe hez lorde of þis hous, herber to craue ?"

[Fol. 102.]
"You are welcome to dwell here as long as you like," replied the porter.
"Ze, Peter," quoth þe porter, " & purely I trowe,[1]

þat ze be, wyze, welcum to won quyle yow lykez."

þen zede þat wyze azayn swyþe,

The draw-bridge is let down,
816 & folke frely hym wyth, to fonge þe knyzt ;

þay let doun þe grete drazt, & derely out zeden,

& kneled doun on her knes vpon þe colde erþe,

To welcum þis ilk wyz, as worþy hom þozt ;

and the gate is opened wide to receive him.
820 þay zolden hym þe brode zate, zarked vp wyde,

& he hem raysed rekenly, & rod ouer þe brygge ;

Sere seggez hym sesed by sadel, quel[2] he lyzt,

His horse is well stabled.
Knights and squires bring Gawayne into the hall.
Many a one hastens to take his
& syþen stabeled his stede stif men in-noze.

824 Knyztez & swyerez comen doun þenne,

For to bryng þis burne[3] wyth blys in-to halle ;

Quen he hef vp his helme, þer hized in-noghe

---

[1] trowoe, MS. [2] quyle (?) or (quen ?). [3] buurne, MS.

For to hent hit at his honde, þe hende to seruen,
828 His bronde & his blasoun boþe þay token.
 þen haylsed he ful hendly þo haþeleȝ vch one,
 & mony proud mon þer presed, þat prynce to honour;
 Alle hasped in his heȝ wede to halle þay hym wonnen,
832 þer fayre fyre vpon flet fersly brenned.
 þenne þe lorde of þe lede louteȝ fro his chambre,
 For to mete wyth menske þe mon on þe flor;
 He sayde, " ȝe ar welcum to welde as yow lykeȝ,
836 þat here is, al is yowre awen, to haue at yowre wylle
   & welde."
  "Graunt mercy," quoth Gawayn,
  "þer kryst hit yow for-ȝelde,"
840 As frekeȝ þat semed fayn,
  Ayþer oþer in armeȝ con felde.

helmet and
sword.

The lord of the
country bids him
welcome,

and they embrace
each other.

XV.

Gawayn glyȝt on þe gome þat godly hym gret,
 & þuȝt hit a bolde burne þat þe burȝ aȝte,
844 A hoge haþel for þe noneȝ, & of hyghe elde;[1]
 Brode bryȝt watȝ his berde, & al beuer hwed,
 Sturne stif on þe stryþþe on stalworth schonkeȝ,
 Felle face as þe fyre, & fre of hys speche;
848 & wel hym semed for soþe, as þe segge þuȝt,
 To lede a lortschyp in lee of leudeȝ ful gode.
 þe lorde hym charred to a chambre, & chefly[2] cumaundeȝ
 To delyuer hym a leude, hym loȝly to serue;
852 & þere were boun at his bode burneȝ in-noȝe,
 þat broȝt hym to a bryȝt boure, þer beddyng watȝ noble,
 Of cortynes of clene sylk, wyth cler golde hemmeȝ,
 & couertoreȝ ful curious, with comlych paneȝ,
856 Of bryȝt blaunnier a-boue enbrawded bisydeȝ,
 Rudeleȝ rennande on ropeȝ, red golde ryngeȝ,
 Tapyteȝ tyȝt to þe woȝe, of tuly & tars,

Gawayne looks
on his host;
a big bold one he
seemed.

Beaver-hued was
his broad beard,

and his face as
"fell as the fire."

[Fol. 102b.]
The lord leads
Gawayne to a
chamber, and as-
signs him a page
to wait upon him.

In this bright
bower was noble
bedding;

The curtains were
of pure silk with
golden hems;

Tarsic tapestries
covered the walls
and the floor.

---

[1] eldee, MS.   [2] clesly, MS.

& vnder fete, on þe flet, of folȝande sute.

860 Þer he watȝ dispoyled, wyth specheȝ of myerþe,

Þe burn of his bruny, & of his bryȝt wedeȝ;

Ryche robes ful rad renkkeȝ hem¹ broȝten,

For to charge, and to chaunge, & chose of the best.

864 Sone as he on hent, & happed þer-inne,

Þat sete on hym² semly, wyth saylande skyrteȝ,

Þe ver by his uisage verayly hit semed

Wel neȝ to vche haþel alle on hwes,

868 Lowande & lufly, alle his lymmeȝ vnder,

Þat a comloker knyȝt neuer kryst made,

hem þoȝt;

Wheþen in worlde he were,

872 Hit semed as he myȝt

Be prynce with-outen pere,

In felde þer felle men fyȝt.

XVI.

A cheyer by-fore þe chemné, þer charcole brenned,

876 Watȝ grayþed for syr Gawan, grayþely with cloþeȝ,

Whyssynes vpon queldepoyntes, þa[t] koynt wer boþe;

& þenne a mere mantyle watȝ on þat mon cast,

Of a broun bleeaunt, enbrauded ful ryche,

880 & fayre furred wyth-inne with felleȝ of þe best,

Alle of ermyn in erde, his hode of þe same;

& he sete in þat settel semlych ryche,

& achaufed hym chefly,³ & þenne his cher mended.

884 Sone watȝ telded vp a tapit, on tresteȝ ful fayre,

Clad wyth a clene cloþe, þat cler quyt schewed,

Sanap, & salure, & syluer-in sponeȝ;

Þe wyȝe wesche at his wylle, & went to his mete.

888 Seggeȝ hym serued semly in-noȝe,

Wyth sere sewes & sete,⁴ sesounde of þe best,

---

¹ hym (?).   ² hyn, in MS.   ³ cefly, in MS.   ⁴ swete (?).

Double felde, as hit falleȝ, & fele kyn fischeȝ;

Summe baken in bred, summe brad on þe gledeȝ,

892 Summe soþen, summe in sewe, sauered with spyces,

& ay sawes¹ so sleȝeȝ, þat þe segge lyked.

þe freke calde hit a fest ful frely & ofte,

Ful hendely, quen alle þe haþeles re-hayted hym at oneȝ

896   as hende ;

"Þis penaunce now ȝe take,

& eft hit schal amende ;"

Þat mon much merþe con make,

900   For wyn in his hed þat wende.

with fish baked and broiled, or boiled and seasoned with spices.

He calls it a full noble feast,

and much mirth he makes, for the wine is in his head.

XVII.

Þenne watȝ spyed & spured vpon spare wyse,

Bi preue poynteȝ of þat prynce, put to hym-seluen,

Þat he be-knew cortaysly of þe court þat he were,

904 Þat aþel Arthure þe hende haldeȝ hym one,

Þat is þe ryche ryal kyng of þe rounde table ;

& hit watȝ Wawen hym-self þat in þat won sytteȝ,

Comen to þat krystmasse, as case hym þen lymped.

908 When þe lorde hade lerned þat he þe leude hade,

Loude laȝed he þerat, so lef hit hym þoȝt,

& alle þe men in þat mote maden much joye,

To apere in his presense prestly þat tyme,

912 Þat alle prys, & prowes, & pured þewes

Apendes to hys persoun, & praysed is euer,

Byfore alle men vpon molde, his mensk is þe most.

Vch segge ful softly sayde to his fere,

916 "Now schal we semlych se sleȝteȝ of þeweȝ,

& þe teccheles termes of talkyng noble,

Wich spede is in speche, vnspurd may we lerne,

Syn we haf fonged þat fyne fader of nurture ;

920 God hatȝ geuen vus his grace godly for soþe,

Þat such a gest as Gawan grauȝteȝ vus to haue,

Sir Gawayne, in answer to questions put to him,

tells the prince that he is of Arthur's court.

When this was made known,

great was the joy in the hall.

Each one said softly to his mate,

"Now we shall see courteous manners and hear noble speech,

for we have amongst us the 'father of nurture.'

¹ sewes (?).

When burneȝ blyþe of his burþe schal sitte
   & synge.

924 In menyng of manereȝ mere,

Þis burne now schal vus bryng,

He that may him
hear shall learn of
love-talking."

I hope þat may hym here,

Schal lerne of luf-talkyng."

XVIII.

After dinner the
company go to
the Chapel,

928 Bi þat þe diner watȝ done, & þe dere vp,

Hit watȝ neȝ at þe niyȝt neȝed þe tyme;

Chaplayneȝ to þe chapeles chosen þe gate,

Rungen ful rychely, ryȝt as þay schulden,

to hear the even-
song of the great
season.

932 To þe hersum euensong of þe hyȝe tyde.

Þe lorde loutes þerto, & þe lady als,

In-to a comly closet scyntly ho entreȝ;

Gawan glydeȝ ful gay, & gos þeder sone;

936 Þe lorde laches hym by þe lappe, & ledeȝ hym to sytte,

& couþly hym knoweȝ, & calleȝ hym his nome,

& sayde he watȝ þe welcomest wyȝe of þe worlde;

The lord of the
castle and Sir
Gawayne sit to-
gether during
service.

& he hym þonkked þroly, & ayþer halched oþer,

940 & seten soberly samen þe seruise-quyle;

Þenne lyst þe lady to loke on þe knyȝt.

His wife, accom-
panied by her
maids, leaves her
seat.

Þenne com ho of hir closet, with mony cler burdeȝ,

Ho watȝ þe fayrest in felle, of flesche & of lyre,

944 & of compas, & colour, & costes of alle other,

She appeared
even fairer than
Guenever.

& wener þen Wenore, as þe wyȝe þoȝt.

An older lady (an
ancient one she
seemed) led her
by the hand.

He ches purȝ þe chaunsel, to cheryche þat hende;

An oþer lady hir lad bi þe lyft honde,

948 Þat watȝ alder þen ho, an auncian hit semed,

& heȝly honowred with haþeles aboute.

Very unlike were
these two.

Bot vn-lyke on to loke þo ladyes were,

If the young one
was fair the other
was yellow,

For if þe ȝonge watȝ ȝep, ȝolȝe watȝ þat oþer;

952 Riche red on þat on rayled ay quere,

and had rough
and wrinkled
cheeks.

Rugh ronkled chekeȝ þat oþer on rolled;

Kerchofes of þat on wyth mony cler perleȝ

The younger had
breast and throat

Hir brest & hir bryȝt þrote bare displayed,

956 Schon schyrer þen snawe, þat scheder[1] on hilleȝ;

 þat oþer wyth a gorger watȝ gered ouer þe swyre,

 Chymbled ouer hir blake chyn with mylk-quyte vayles,

 Hir frount folden in sylk, enfoubled ay quere,

960 Toret & treleted[2] with tryfleȝ aboute,

 þat noȝt watȝ bare of þat burde bot þe blake broȝes,

 þe tweyne yȝen, & þe nase, þe naked lyppeȝ,

 & þose were soure to se, & sellyly blered;

964 A mensk lady on molde mon may hir calle,

  for gode;

 Hir body watȝ schort & þik,

 Hir buttokeȝ bay & brode,

968 More lykker-wys on to lyk,

 Watȝ þat scho hade on lode.

"bare display-ed."

The ancient one exposed only her "black brows," [Fol. 104.]

her two eyes, nose, and naked lips, all sour and bleared,

Her body was short and thick; her buttocks broad and round.

XIX.

 When Gawayn glyȝt on þat gay, þat graciously loked,

 Wyth leue laȝt of þe lorde he went hem aȝaynes;

972 þe alder he haylses, heldande ful lowe,

 þe loueloker he lappeȝ a lyttel in armeȝ,

 He kysses hir comlyly, & knyȝtly he meleȝ;

 þay kallen hym of a quoyntaunce, & he hit quyk askeȝ

976 To be her seruaunt sothly, if hem-self lyked.

 þay tan hym bytwene hem, wyth talkyng hym leden

 To chambre, to chemné, & chefly þay asken

 Spyceȝ, þat vn-sparely men speded hom to bryng,

980 & þe wynne-lych wyne þer-with vche tyme.

 þe lorde luflych aloft lepeȝ ful ofte,

 Mynned merthe to be made vpon mony syþeȝ.

 Hent heȝly of his hode, & on a spere henged,

984 & wayned hom to wynne þe worchip þer-of,

 þat most myrþe myȝt mene[3] þat crystenmas whyle;

 "& I schal fonde, bi my fayth, to fylter wyth þe best,

 Er me wont þe wedeȝ, with help of my frendeȝ."

With permission of the lord,

Sir Gawayne sa-lutes the elder,

but the younger he kisses,

and begs to be her servant.

To chamber all go,

where spices and wine are served.

The lord takes off his hood and places it on a spear.

He who makes most mirth is to win it.

---

[1] schedes (?). [2] treieted (?). [3]. mene (?).

988 Þus wyth laȝande loteȝ þe lorde hit tayt[1] makeȝ,

Night approach-
es, and then

For to glade syr Gawayn with gomneȝ in halle

        þat nyȝt;

Til þat hit watȝ tyme,

992   Þe kyng comaundet lyȝt,

Sir Gawayne
takes his leave
and retires to
rest.

Syr Gawen his leue con nyme,

   & to his bed hym diȝt.

XX.

On Christmas
morn,

On þe morne, as vch mon myneȝ þat tyme,

joy reigns in
every dwelling in
the world.
So did it in the
castle where our
knight abode.
[Fol. 104b.]

996 Þat dryȝtyn for oure destyné to deȝe watȝ borne,

Wele waxeȝ in vche a won in worlde, for his sake ;

So did hit þere on þat day, þurȝ dayntes mony ;

Boþe at mes & at mele, messes ful quaynt

1000 Derf men vpon dece drest of þe best.

The lord and "the
old ancient wife"
sit together.

Þe olde auncian wyf heȝest ho sytteȝ ;

Þe lorde lufly her by lent, as I trowe ;

Gawayne sits by
the wife of his
host.

Gawan & þe gay burde to-geder þay seten,

1004 Euen in-myddeȝ, as þe messe metely come ;

& syþen þurȝ al þe sale, as hem best semed,

It were too tedi-
ous to tell of the
meat, the mirth,
or the joy that
abounded every-
where.

Bi vche grome at his degre grayþely watȝ serued.

Þer watȝ mete, þer watȝ myrþe, þer watȝ much ioye,

1008 Þat for to telle þerof hit me tene were,

& to poynte hit ȝet I pyned me perauenture ;

Gawayne and his
beautiful com-
panion derive
much comfort
from each other's
conversation.

Bot ȝet I wot þat Wawen & þe wale burde

Such comfort of her cōpaynye caȝten to-geder,

1012 Þurȝ her dere dalyaunce of her derne wordeȝ,

Wyth clene cortays carp, closed fro fylþe ;

& hor play watȝ passande vche prynce gomen,

        in vayres ;

Trumpets and
nakers give forth
their sounds.

1016   Trumpeȝ & nakerys,

Much pypyng þer repayres,

Vche mon tented hys,

& þay two tented þayres.

            [1] layt (?).

XXI.

1020 Much dut watȝ þer dryuen þat day & þat oþer,   *Great was the joy for three days.*
 & þe þryd as þro þronge in þerafter;
 Þe ioye of sayn[t] Ioneȝ day watȝ gentyle to here,   *St. John's-day was the last of Christmas festival.*
 & watȝ þe last of þe layk, leudeȝ þer þoȝten.
1024 Þer wer gestes to go vpon þe gray morne,
 For-þy wonderly þay woke, & þe wyn dronken,
 Daunsed ful dreȝly wyth dere caroleȝ;
 At þe last, when hit watȝ late, þay lachen her leue,   *On the morrow many of the guests took their departure from the castle.*
1028 Vchon to wende on his way, þat watȝ wyȝe stronge.
 Gawan gef hym god-day, þe god mon hym lachcheȝ,
 Ledes hym to his awen chambre, þe chymné bysyde,
 & þere he draȝeȝ hym on-dryȝe, & derely hym þonkkeȝ,   *Sir Gawayne is thanked by his host for the honour and pleasure of his visit.*
1032 Of þe wynne worschip &¹ he hym wayned hade,
 As to honour his hous on þat hyȝe tyde,
 & enbelyse his burȝ with his bele chere.
 "I-wysse syr, quyl I leue, me worþeȝ þe bettor,
1036 Þat Gawayn hatȝ ben my gest, at goddeȝ awen fest." [Fol. 105.]
 "Grant merci² syr," quoth Gawayn, "in god fayth
  hit is yowreȝ,
 Al þe honour is your awen, þe heȝe kyng yow ȝelde;
 & I am wyȝe at your wylle, to worch youre hest,
1040 As I am halden þer-to, in hyȝe & in loȝe,
  bi riȝt."
 Þe lorde fast can hym payne,   *He endeavours to keep the knight at his court.*
 To holde lenger þe knyȝt,
1044 To hym answreȝ Gawayn,
 Bi non way þat he myȝt.

XXII.

 Then frayned þe freke ful fayre at him-seluen,   *He desires to know what had driven Sir Gawayne from Arthur's court before the end of the Christmas holidays.*
 Quat derne³ dede had hym dryuen, at þat dere tyme,
1048 So kenly fro þe kyngeȝ kourt to kayre al his one,
 Er þe halidayeȝ holly were halet out of toun?

 ¹ þat (?).   ² nerci, in MS.   ³ derue (?).

3

The knight replies that "a high errand and a hasty one" had forced him to leave the court.

"For soþe syr," quoth þe segge, "ȝe sayn bot þe trawþe;

A heȝe ernde & a hasty me hade fro þo woneȝ,

1052 For I am sumned my selfe to sech to a place,

I wot[1] in worlde wheder warde to wende, hit to fynde ;

I noke, bot if I hit negh myȝt on nwȝeres morne,

For alle þe londe in-wyth Logres, so me oure lorde help!

1056 For-þy, syr, þis enquest I require yow here,

He asks his host whether he has ever heard of the Green Chapel,

þat ȝe me telle with trawthe, if euer ȝe tale herde

Of þe grene chapel, quere hit on grounde stondeȝ,

& of þe knyȝt þat hit kepes, of colour of grene ?

1060 þer watȝ stabled bi statut a steuen vus by-twene,

for he has to be there on New Year's-day.

To mete þat mon at þat mere, ȝif I myȝt last ;

& of þat ilk nwȝere bot neked now wonteȝ,

& I wolde loke on þat lede, if god me let wolde,

1064 Gladloker, bi goddeȝ sun, þen any god welde !

For-þi, I-wysse, bi ȝowre wylle, wende me bi-houes,

He would as lief die as fail in his errand.

Naf I now to busy bot bare þre dayeȝ,

& me als fayn to falle feye as fayly of myyn ernde."

The prince tells Sir Gawayne that he will teach him the way.

1068 þenne laȝande quoth þe lorde, "now leng þe by-houes,

For I schal teche yow to-þa[t] terme bi þe tymeȝ ende,

þe grene chapayle vpon grounde, greue yow no more ;

Bot ȝe schal be in yowre bed, burne, at þyn ese,

1072 Quyle forth dayeȝ, & ferk on þe fyrst of þe ȝere,

[Fol. 105b.]

& cum to þat merk at mydmorn, to make quat yow likeȝ

in spenne ;

Dowelleȝ whyle new ȝeres daye,

1076 & rys, & raykeȝ þenne,

The Green Chapel is not more than two miles from the castle.

Mon schal yow sette in waye,

Hit is not two myle henne."

XXIII.

Then was Gawayne glad,

þenne watȝ Gawan ful glad, & gomenly he laȝed,—

1080 "Now I þonk yow þryuandely þurȝ alle oþer þynge,

and consents to tarry awhile at the castle.

Now acheued is my chaunce, I schal at your wylle

Dowelle, & elleȝ do quat ȝe demen."

[1] not (?).

þenne sesed hym þe syre, & set hym bysyde,

1084 Let þe ladieȝ be fette, to lyke hem þe better ;

þer watȝ seme solace by hem-self stille ;

þe lorde let for luf loteȝ so myry,

As wyȝ þat wolde of his wyte, ne wyst quat he myȝt.

1088 þenne he carped to þe knyȝt, criande loude,

"ȝe han demed to do þe dede þat I bidde ;

Wyl ȝe halde þis hes[t] here at þys oneȝ ?"

"ȝe syr, for-soþe," sayd þe segge trwe,

1092 "Whyl I byde in yowre borȝe, be bayn to ȝow[r]e

hest."

"For ȝe haf trauayled," quoth þe tulk, "towen fro ferre,

& syþen waked me wyth, ȝe arn not wel waryst,

Nauþer of sostnaunce ne of slepe, soþly I knowe ;

1096 ȝe schal lenge in your lofte, & lyȝe in your ese,

To morn quyle þe messe-quyle, & to mete wende,

When ȝe wyl, wyth my wyf, þat wyth yow schal sitte,

& comfort yow with compayny, til I to cort torne,

1100   ȝe lende ;

& I schal erly ryse,

On huntyng wyl I wende."

Gauayn granteȝ alle þyse,

1104 Hym heldande, as þe hende.

The ladies are brought in to solace him.

The lord of the castle asks the knight to grant him one request ;

That he will stay in his chamber during mass time,

and then go to meat with his hostess.

Gawayne accedes to his request.

XXIV.

"ȝet firre," quoth þe freke, "a forwarde we make ;

Quat-so-euer I wynne in þe wod, hit worþeȝ to youreȝ,

& quat chek so ȝe acheue, chaunge me þer-forne ;

1108 Swete, swap we so, sware with trawþe,

Queþer, leude, so lymp lere oþer better."

"Bi god," quoth Gawayn þe gode, "I grant þer-tylle,

& þat yow lyst for to layke, lef hit me þynkes.

1112 "Who bryngeȝ vus þis beuerage, þis bargayn is

maked :"

So sayde þe lorde of þat lede ; þay laȝed vchone,

"Whatsoever," says the host, "I win in the wood shall be yours,

and what check you achieve shall be mine."

[Fol. 106.]

A bargain is made between them.

Þay dronken, & daylyeden, & dalten vnty₃tel,[1]
Þise lorde₃ and ladye₃, quyle þat hem lyked;
1116 & syþen wіth frenkysch fare & fele fayre lote₃
Þay stoden, & stemed, & stylly speken,
Kysten ful comlyly, & ka₃ten her leue.

Night approaches and each "to his bed was brought at the last." Wіth mony leude ful ly₃t, & lemande torches,
1120 Vche burne to his bed wat₃ bro₃t at þe laste,
ful softe ;
To bed ₃et er þay ₃ede,
Recorded couenaunte₃ ofte ;
1124 Þe olde lorde of þat leude,[2]
Cowþe wel halde layk a-lofte.

[FYTTE THE THIRD.]

I.

Before day-break folks uprise, FUL erly bifore þe day þe folk vp-rysen,
Gestes þat go wolde, hor grome₃ þay calden,
saddle their horses, and truss their mails. 1128 & þay busken vp bilyue, blonkke₃ to sadel,
Tyffen he[r] takles, trussen her males,
Richen hem þe rychest, to ryde alle arayde,
Lepen vp ly₃tly, lachen her brydeles,
Each goes where it pleases him best. 1132 Vche wy₃e on his way, þer hym wel lyked.
The noble lord of the land arrays himself for riding. Þe leue lorde of þe londe wat₃ not þe last,
A-rayed for þe rydyng, wіth renkke₃ ful mony;
He eats a sop hastily and goes to mass. Ete a sop hastyly, when he hade herde masse,
1136 Wіth bugle to bent felde he buske₃ by-lyue;
Before day-light he and his men are on their horses. By þat þat any day-ly₃t lemed vpon erþe,
He wіth his haþeles on hy₃e horsses weren.
Then the hounds are called out and coupled. Þenne þise cacheres þat couþe, cowpled hor hounde₃,
1140 Vnclosed þe kenel dore, & calde hem þer-oute,
Three short notes are blown by the bugles. Blwe bygly in bugle₃ þre bare mote ;
Braches bayed þerfore, & breme noyse maked,

---

[1] vntyl ny₃te (?).   [2] lede (?).

& þay chastysed, & charred, on chasy*n*g þat went;

1144 A hundreth of hunt*e*res, as I haf herde telle,

of þe best;

To trystors vewters ȝod,

Couples huntes of kest,

1148 Þ*er* ros for blasteȝ gode,

Gret rurd i*n* þat forest.

Marginal notes: A hundred hunters join in the chase. / To the stations the "fewters" go, / [Fol. 106b.] / and the dogs are cast off.

II.

At þe fyrst quethe of þe quest quaked þe wylde;

Der drof i*n* þe dale, doted for drede,

1152 Hiȝed to þe hyȝe, bot het*er*ly þay were

Restayed w*ith* þe stablye, þat stoutly ascryed;

Þay let þe hertteȝ haf þe gate, w*ith* þe hyȝe hedes,

Þe breme bukkeȝ also, w*ith* hor brode paumeȝ;

1156 For þe fre lorde hade defende i*n* fermysou*n* tyme,

Þat þ*er* schulde no mon mene[1] to þe male dere.

Þe hindeȝ were halden i*n*, w*ith* hay & war,

Þe does dryuen w*ith* gret dyn to þe depe sladeȝ;

1160 Þer myȝt mon se, as þay slypte, slenty*n*g of arwes,

At vche [þat] wende vnder wande wapped a flone,

Þat bigly bote on þe brou*n*, w*ith* ful brode hedeȝ,

What! þay brayen, & bleden, bi bonkkeȝ þay deȝen.

1164 & ay rachches i*n* a res radly hem folȝes,

Hunt*e*reȝ wyth hyȝe horne hasted hem aft*er*,

Wyth such a crakkande kry, as klyffes haden bruste*n*;

What wylde so at-waped wyȝes þat schotten,

1168 Watȝ al to-raced & rent, at þe resayt.

Bi þay were tened at þe hyȝe, and taysed to þe wattreȝ,

Þe ledeȝ were so lerned at þe loȝe trysteres,

& þe gre-hou*n*deȝ so grete, þat geten hem bylyue,

1172 & hem to fylched, as fast as frekeȝ myȝt loke,

þer ryȝt.

Þe lorde for blys abloy

Ful oft con lau*n*ce & lyȝt,

Marginal notes: Roused by the clamour the deer rush to the heights, / but are soon driven back. / The male deer and bucks are allowed to pass, / but the hinds and does are driven back to the shades. / As they fly they are shot by the bowmen. / The hounds and the hunters, with a loud cry, follow in pursuit. / Those that escaped the arrows are killed by the hounds. / The lord waxes joyful in the chase,

[1] meue?

which lasted till 1176
the approach of
night.

> & drof þat day wyth Ioy.
> Thus to þe derk nyȝt.

III.

All this time Ga-
wayne lies a-bed,

> Þus laykeȝ þis lorde by lynde wodeȝ eueȝ.
> & G. þe god mon, in gay bed lygeȝ,

under "cover- 1180
ture full clear."

> Lurkkeȝ quyl þe day-lyȝt lemed on þe wowes,
> Vnder couertour ful clere, cortyned aboute;
> & as in slomcryng he slode, sleȝly he herde

He hears a noise
at his door.

> A littel dyn at his dor, & derfly vpon;

1184

> & he heueȝ vp his hed out of þe cloþes,

[Fol. 107.]

> A corner of þe cortyn he caȝt vp a lyttel,
> & wayteȝ warly þider-warde, quat hit be myȝt.

A lady, the love-
liest to behold,
enters softly.

> Hit watȝ þe ladi, loflyest to be-holde,

1188

> Þat droȝ þe dor after hir ful dernly[1] & stylle,

She approaches
the bed.

> & boȝed to-warde þe bed; & þe burne schamed,
> & layde hym doun lystyly, & let as he slepte.

Gawayne pre-
tends to be asleep.

> & ho stepped stilly, & stel to his bedde,

The lady casts up 1192
the curtain and
sits on the bed-
side.

> Kest vp þe cortyn, & creped with-inne,
> & set hir ful softly on þe bed-syde,
> & lenged þere selly longe, to loke quen he wakened.
> Þe lede lay lurked a ful longe quyle,

Gawayne has 1196
much wonder
thereat.

> Compast in his concience to quat þat cace myȝt
> Mene oþer amount, to meruayle hym þoȝt;
> Bot ȝet he sayde in hym-self, "more semly hit were
> To aspye wyth my spelle [in] space quat ho wolde."

He rouses him- 1200
self up,

> Þen he wakenede, & wroth, & to hir warde torned,

unlocks his eyes,
and looks as if he
were astonished.

> & vn-louked his yȝe-lyddeȝ, & let as hym wondered,
> & sayned hym, as bi his saȝe þe sauer to worthe,
> with hande;

1204

> Wyth chynne & cheke ful swete,
> Boþe quit & red in-blande,
> Ful lufly con ho lete,
> Wyth lyppeȝ smal laȝande.

[1] deruly (?).

IV.

1208 "God moroun, syr Gawayn," sayde þat fayr lady,
  "Ʒe ar a sleper vn-slyʒe, þat mon may slyde hider;
  Now ar ʒe tan astyt, bot true vus may schape,
  I schal bynde yow in your bedde, þat be ʒe trayst:"
1212 Al laʒande þe lady lanced þo bourdeʒ.
  "Goud moroun gaye,"¹ quoth Gawayn þe blyþe,
  "Me schal worþe at your wille, & þat me wel lykeʒ,
  For I ʒelde me ʒederly, & ʒeʒe after grace,
1216 & þat is þe best, be my dome, for me by-houeʒ nede;"
  & þus he bourded a-ʒayn with mony a blyþe laʒter.
  "Bot wolde ʒe, lady louely, þen leue me grante,
  & deprece your prysoun,² & pray hym to ryse,
1220 I wolde boʒe of þis bed, & busk me better,
  I schulde keuer þe more comfort to karp yow wyth."
  "Nay, for soþe, beau syr," sayd þat swete,
  "Ʒe schal not rise of your bedde, I rych yow better,
1224 I schal happe yow here þat oþer half als,
  & syþen karp wyth my knyʒt þat I kaʒt haue;
  For I wene wel, I-wysse, syr Wawen ʒe are,
  þat alle þe worlde worchipeʒ, quere-so ʒe ride;
1228 Your honour, your hendelayk is hendely praysed
  With lordeʒ, wyth ladyes, with alle þat lyf bere.
  & now ʒe ar here, I-wysse, and we bot oure one;
  My lorde & his ledeʒ ar on lenþe faren,
1232 Oþer burneʒ in her bedde, & my burdeʒ als,
  þe dor drawen, & dit with a derf haspe;
  & syþen I haue in þis hous hym þat al lykeʒ,
  I schal ware my whyle wel, quyl hit lasteʒ,
1236   with tale;
  Ʒe ar welcum to my cors,
  Yowre awen won to wale,
  Me be-houeʒ of fyne force,
1240   Your seruaunt be & schale."

¹ This word is doubtful in the MS.   ² prysouner (?).

Side notes:
"Good morrow," says the lady, "ye are a careless sleeper to let one enter thus.
I shall bind you in your bed, of that be ye sure."
"Good morrow," says the knight, "I am well pleased to be at your service;
but permit me to rise and dress myself."
[Fol. 107b.] "Nay, beau sir," said that sweet one,
"I shall hold talk with you here.
I know well that you are Gawayne that all the world worships.
We are by ourselves;
My lord and his men are far off. Other men are in their beds, so are my maidens. The door is safely closed. Since I have him in house that everyone likes, I shall use my time well while it lasts.
Ye are welcome to my body.
I shall be your servant."

V.

"In god fayth," quoth Gawayn, "gayn hit me þynkkeȝ,

þaȝ I be not now he þat ȝe of speken;

"I am unwor-
thy," says Sir
Gawayne, "to
reach to such
reverence as ye
rehearse.
To reche to such reuerence as ȝe reherce here

1244 I am wyȝe vn-worthy, I wot wel my-seluen;

Bi god, I were glad, & yow god þoȝt,

I shall be glad,
however, to
please you by
word or service."
At saȝe oþer at seruyce þat I sette myȝt

To þe plesaunce of your prys, hit were a pure ioye."

1248 "In god fayth, syr Gawayn," quoth þe gay lady,

"þe prys & þe prowes þat pleseȝ al oþer,

If I hit lakked, oþer set at lyȝt, hit were littel daynté;

"There are la-
dies," says his
visitor, "who
would prefer thy
company
Bot hit ar ladyes in-noȝe, þat leuer wer nowþe

1252 Haf þe hende in hor holde, as I þe habbe here,

To daly with derely your daynté wordeȝ,

Keuer hem comfort, & colen her careȝ,

to much of the
gold that they
possess."
þen much of þe garysoun oþer golde þat¹ þay hauen;

1256 Bot I loune² þat ilk lorde þat þe lyfte haldeȝ,

I haf hit holly in my honde þat al desyres,

þurȝe grace."

Scho made hym so gret chere,

[Fol. 108.] 1260 þat watȝ so fayr of face,

The knight an-
swers the lady's
questions.
þe knyȝt with speches skere,

A[n]swared to vche a cace.

VI.

Gawayne tells
her that he pre-
fers her conver-
sation before that
of all others.
"Madame," quoth þe myry mon, "Mary yow ȝelde,

1264 For I haf founden, in god fayth, yowre fraunchis nobele,

& oþer ful much of oþer folk fongen hor dedeȝ;

Bot þe daynté þat þay delen for my disert nysen,

Hit is þe worchyp of your-self, þat noȝt bot wel conneȝ."

The lady declares
by Mary,
1268 "Bi Mary," quoth þe menskful, "me þynk hit anoþer;

For were I worth al þe wone of wymmen alyue,

that were she
about to choose
her a lord,
& al þe wele of þe worlde were in my honde,

& I schulde chepen & chose, to cheue me a lorde,

¹ þat þat, in MS.   ² louie or loune (?).

1272 For þe costes þat I haf knowen vpon þe knyȝt here,
  Of bewté, & debonerté, & blyþe semblaunt,
  & þat I haf er herkkened, & halde hit here trwee, *she would select Gawayne before anyman on earth.*
  Þer schulde no freke vpon folde bifore yow be chosen."
1276 "I-wysse, worþy," quoth þe wyȝe, "ȝe haf waled wel
    better,
  Bot I am proude of þe prys þat ȝe put on me, *Gawayne tells her that he will become her own knight and faithful servant.*
  & soberly your seruaunt my souerayn I holde yow,
  & yowre knyȝt I be-com, & kryst yow for-ȝelde."
1280 Þus þay meled of much-quat, til myd-morn paste,
  & ay þe lady let lyk, a¹ hym loued mych;
  þe freke ferde with defence, and feted ful fayre.
  Þaȝ I were burde bryȝtest, þe burde in mynde hade, *The remembrance of his adventure prevents him from thinking of love.*
1284 Þe lasse luf in his lode, for lur þat he soȝt,
      boute hone;
    þe dunte þat schulde² hym deue,
    & nedeȝ hit most be done;
1288   þe lady þenn spek of leue, *The lady takes leave of Sir Gawayne.*
    He grauted hir ful sone.

VII.

Þenne ho gef hym god-day, & wyth a glent laȝed, *With a laughing glance, she says,*
  & as ho stod, ho stonyed hym wyth ful stor wordeȝ:
1292 "Now he þat spedeȝ vche spech, þis disport ȝelde yow! *"I am doubtful whether ye be Gawayne.*
  Bot þat ȝe be Gawan, hit gotȝ in mynde."
  "Quer-fore?" quoth þe freke, & freschly he askeȝ,
  Ferde lest he hade fayled in fourme of his castes;
1296 Bot þe burde hym blessed, & bi þis skyl sayde,
  "So god as Gawayn gaynly is halden, *[Fol. 108b.]*
  & cortaysye is closed so clene in hym-seluen,
  Couth not lyȝtly haf lenged so long wyth a lady, *Were it he, surely, ere this, he would have craved a kiss."*
1300 Bot he had craued a cosse, bi his courtaysye,
  Bi sum towch of summe tryfle, at sum taleȝ ende."
  Þen quoth Wowen, "I-wysse, worþe as yow lykeȝ, *"I shall kiss," says the knight,*

¹ ande (?).   ² sclulde, in MS.

"at your com-
mandment."

I schal kysse at your comaundement, as a knyȝt falleȝ,
1304 & fire[1] lest he displese yow, so[2] plede hit no more."

With that the
lady catches him
in her arms and
kisses him.

Ho comes nerre with þat, & cacheȝ hym in armeȝ,
Louteȝ luflych adoun, & þe leude kysseȝ;
þay comly bykennen to kryst ayþer oþer;
1308 Ho dos hir forth at þe dore, with-outen dyn more.

& he ryches hym to ryse, & rapes hym sone,

Gawayne then
rises and goes to
mass.

Clepes to his chamberlayn, choses his wede,
Boȝeȝ forth, quen he watȝ boun, blyþely to masse,
1312 & þenne he meued to his mete, þat menskly hym keped,

He makes mirth
all day till the
moon rises,

& made myry al day til þe mone rysed,
                    with game;
                 With[3] neuer freke fayrer fonge,

between the "two
dames," the older
and the younger.

1316   Bitwene two so dyngne dame,
             þe alder & þe ȝonge,
             Much solace set þay same.

                    VIII.

Meanwhile the
lord of the land
and his men hunt
in woods and
heaths.

And ay þe lorde of þe londe is lent on his gamneȝ,
1320 To hunt in holteȝ & heþe, at hyndeȝ barayne,
Such a sowme he þer slowe bi þat þe sunne heldet,
Of dos & of oþer dere, to deme were wonder.
þenne fersly þay flokked in folk at þe laste,

Quickly of the
killed a "quarry"
they make.

1324 & quykly of þe quelled dere a querré þay maked;
þe best boȝed þerto, with burneȝ in-noghe,

Then they set
about breaking
the deer.

Gedered þe grattest of gres þat þer were,
& didden hem derely vndo, as þe dede askeȝ;

They take away
the assay or fat,

1328 Serched hem at þe asay, summe þat þer were,
Two fyngeres þay fonde of þe fowlest of alle;

then they slit the
slot and remove
the erber.
They afterwards
rip the four limbs
and rend off the
hide.

Syþen þay slyt þe slot, sesed þe erber,
Schaued wyth a scharp knyf, & þe schyre knitten;
1332 Syþen rytte þay þe foure lymmes, & rent of þe hyde,

They next open
the belly and take
out the bowels.
[Fol. 109.]

þen brek þay þe bale, þe baleȝ out token,
Lystily forlancyng, & here of þe knot;

---

[1] fere (?).   [2] fo, in MS.   [3] Was (?) Nas (?).

Þay gryped to þe gargulun, & grayþely departed

1336 Þe wesaunt fro þe wynt-hole, & walt out þe gutteȝ;

Þen scher þay out þe schuldereȝ wíth her scharp knyueȝ,

Haled hem by a lyttel hole, to haue hole sydes;

Syþen britned þay þe brest, & brayden hit in twynne,

1340 & eft at þe gargulun bigyneȝ on þenne,

Ryueȝ hit vp radly, ryȝt to þe byȝt,

Voydeȝ out þe a-vanters, & verayly þer-after

Alle þe rymeȝ by þe rybbeȝ radly þay lance ;

1344 So ryde þay of by resoun bi þe rygge boneȝ,

Euenden to þe haunche, þat henged alle samen,

& heuen hit vp al hole, & hwen hit of þere,

& þat þay neme for þe noumbles, bi nome as I trowe,

1348 bi kynde;

Bi þe byȝt al of þe þyȝes,

Þe lappeȝ þay lance bi-hynde,

To hewe hit in two þay hyȝes,

1352 Bi þe bak-bon to vnbynde.

Side notes:

They then separate the *weasand* from the wind-hole and throw out the guts.

The shoulders are cut out, and the breast divided in halves.

The *numbles* are next removed.

By the fork of the thighs,

the flaps are hewn in two by the backbone.

IX.

Boþe þe hede & þe hals þay hwen of þenne,

& syþen sunder þay þe sydeȝ swyft fro þe chyne,

& þe corbeles fee þay kest in a greue ;[1]

1356 Þenn þurled þay ayþer þik side þurȝ, bi þe rybbe,

& henged þenne a[y]þer bi hoȝes of þe fourcheȝ,

Vche freke for his fee, as falleȝ for to haue.

Vpon a felle of þe fayre bÙst, fede þay þayr houndes,

1360 Wyth þe lyuer & þe lyȝteȝ, þe leþer of þe pauncheȝ,

& bred baþed in blod, blende þer amongeȝ;

Baldely þay blw prys, bayed þayr rachcheȝ,

Syþen fonge þay her flesche folden to home,

1364 Strakande ful stoutly mony stif moteȝ.

Bi þat þe daylyȝt watȝ done, þe douthe watȝ al wonen

Side notes:

After this the head and neck are cut off, and the sides severed from the chine.

With the liver, lights, and paunches, they feed the hounds.

Then they make for home.

[1] *on* a grene (?).

In-to þe comly castel, þer þe knyȝt bideȝ
ful stille ;

1368   Wyth blys & bryȝt fyr bette,
þe lord iȝ comen þer-tylle,

Gawayne goes
out to meet his
host.

When Gawayn wyth hym mette,
þer watȝ bot wele at wylle.

X.

[Fol. 109b.] 1372 Thenne comaunded þe lorde in þat sale to samen alle þe
meny,

The lord com-
mands all his
household to as-
semble,

Boþe þe ladyes on loghe to lyȝt with her burdes,

and the venison
to be brought be-
fore him.

Bi-fore alle þe folk on þe flette, frekeȝ he beddeȝ
Verayly his venysoun to fech hym byforne ;

He calls Ga-
wayne,

1376 & al godly in gomen Gaway[n] he called,
Techeȝ hym to þe tayles of ful tayt bestes,
Scheweȝ hym þe schyree grece schorne vpon rybbes.

and asks him
whether he does
not deserve much
praise for his suc-
cess in the chase.

"How payeȝ yow þis play? haf I prys wonnen?
1380 Haue I þryuandely þonk þurȝ my craft serued?"
"Ȝe I-wysse," quoth þat oþer wyȝe, "here is wayth
fayrest

On the knight
expressing him-
self satisfied, he
is told to take the
whole according
to a former agree-
ment between
them.

þat I seȝ þis seuen ȝere in sesoun of wynter."
"& al I gif yow, Gawayn," quoth þe gome þenne,
1384 "For by a-corde of couenaunt ȝe craue hit as your
awen."

"þis is soth," quoth þe segge, "I say yow þat ilke,
&[1] I haf worthyly þis woneȝ wyth-inne,

Gawayne gives
the knight a
comely kiss in
return.

I-wysse with as god wylle hit worþeȝ to ȝoureȝ."
1388 He hasppeȝ his fayre hals his armeȝ wyth-inne,
& kysses hym as comlyly as he[2] couþe awyse :
"Tas yow þere my cheuicaunce, I cheued no more,
I wowche hit saf fynly, þaȝ feler hit were."

1392 "Hit is god," quoth þe god mon, "grant mercy þerfore,

His host desires
to know where
he had gotten
such weal.

Hit may be such, hit is þe better, &[1] ȝe me breue wolde
Where ȝe wan þis ilk wele, by wytte of hor[3] seluen?"

---

[1] And = an.   [2] hó, in MS.   [3] your?

"þat watȝ not forward," q*uoth* he, "frayst me no more,
1396 For ȝe haf tan þat yow tydeȝ, trawe ȝe non oþer
          ȝe mowe."

          þay laȝed, & made hem blyþe,
          Wyth loteȝ þat were to lowe,
1400   To soper þay ȝede asswyþe,
          Wyth dayntes nwe in-nowe.

As this does not enter into the covenant, he gets no answer to his question.

They then proceed to supper, where were dainties new and enough.

XI.

          And syþen by þe chymné in chamber þay seten;
          Wyȝeȝ þe walle wyn weȝed to hem oft,
1404 & efte in her bourdyng þay bayþen in þe morn,
          To fylle þe same forwardeȝ þat þay by-fore maden,
          þat chaunce so by-tydeȝ hor cheuysaunce to chaunge,
          What nweȝ so þay nome, at naȝt quen þay metten
1408 þay acorded of þe couenaunteȝ byfore þe court alle ;
          þe beuerage watȝ broȝt forth in bourde at þat tyme ;
          þenne þay louelych leȝten leue at þe last,
          Vche burne to his bedde busked bylyue.
1412 Bi þat þe coke hade croweȝ[1] & cakled bot þryse,
          þe lorde watȝ lopen of his bedde, [&] þe leudeȝ vch one,
          So þat þe mete & þe masse watȝ metely delyuered ;
          þe douthe dressed to þe wod, er any day sprenged,
1416   to chace ;

              Heȝ with hunte & horneȝ,
              þurȝ playneȝ þay passe in space,
              Vn-coupled among þo þorneȝ,
1420   Racheȝ þat ran on race.

By the hearth they sit. Wine is carried round.

Again Sir Gawayne and his host renew their agreement.

[Fol. 110.]
Then they take leave of each other and hasten to bed.
Scarce had the cock cackled thrice when the lord was up.

With his hunters and horns they pursue the chase.

XII.

          Sone þay calle of a quest in aker syde,
          þe hunt re-hayted þe houndeȝ, þat hit fyrst mynged,
          Wylde wordeȝ hym warp wyth a wrast noyce ;
1424 þe howndeȝ þat hit herde, hastid þider swyþe,

The hunters cheer on the hounds,

which fall to the scent forty at once.

[1] crowed (?).

& fellen as fast to þe fuyt, fourty at ones;

þenne such a glauerande glam of gedered rachcheʒ

Ros, þat þe rochereʒ rungen aboute;

1428 Huntereʒ hem hardened with horne & wyth muthe.

þen al in a semblé sweyed to-geder,

Bitwene a flosche in þat fryth, & a foo cragge;

In a knot, bi a clyffe, at þe kerre syde,

1432 þer as þe rogh rocher yn-rydely watʒ fallen,

þay ferden to þe fyndyng, & frekeʒ hem after;

þay vmbe-kesten þe knarre & þe knot boþe,

Wyʒeʒ, whyl þay wysten wel wyt inne hem hit were,

1436 þe best þat þer breued watʒ wyth þe blod houndeʒ.

þenne þay beten on þe buskeʒ, & bede hym vp ryse,

& he vnsoundyly out soʒt seggeʒ ouer-þwert,

On þe sellokest swyn swenged out þere,

1440 Long sythen for[1] þe sounder þat wiʒt for-olde,

For he watʒ b[este] & bor alþer grattest,

[And eu]ere quen he gronyed, þenne greued mony,

For [þre a]t þe fyrst þrast he þryʒt to þe erþe,

1444 & sped [hym] forth good sped, boute spyt mor

Ande þay halowed hyghe ful hyʒe & hay! hay! cryed,

Haden horneʒ to mouþe heterly rechated;

Mony watʒ þe myry mouthe of men & of houndeʒ,

1448 þat buskkeʒ after þis bor, with bost & wyth noyse,

to quelle;

Ful oft he bydeʒ þe baye,

& maymeʒ þe mute Inn-melle,

1452 He hurteʒ of þe houndeʒ, & þay

Ful ʒomerly ʒaùle & ʒelle.

XIII.

Schalkeʒ to schote at hym schowen to þenne,

Haled to hym of her areweʒ, hitten hym oft;

1456 Bot þe poynteʒ payred at þe pyth þat pyʒt in his scheldeʒ,

& þe barbeʒ of his browe bite non wolde,

Side notes:

All come together by the side of a cliff.

They look about on all sides,

and beat on the bushes.

Out there rushes a fierce wild boar.

At the first thrust, he fells three to the ground.

[Fol. 110b.]

Full quickly the hunters pursue him.

However, he attacks the hounds causing them to yowl and yell.

The bowmen send their arrows after this wild swine,

[1] fro. (?).

þaȝ þe schauen schaft schyndered in peceȝ,
þe hede hypped aȝayn, were-so-euer hit hitte ;

1460 Bot quen þe dynteȝ hym dered of her dryȝe strokeȝ,
þen, brayn-wod for bate, on burneȝ he raseȝ,

Hurteȝ hem ful heterly þer he forth hyȝeȝ,

& mony arȝed þerat, & on-lyte droȝen.

1464 Bot þe lorde on a lyȝt horce launces hym after,
As burne bolde vpon bent his bugle he bloweȝ,

He rechated, & r[ode]¹ þurȝ roneȝ ful þyk,
Suande þis wylde swyn til þe sunne schafted.

1468 þis day wyth þis ilk dede þay dryuen on þis wyse,

Whyle oure luflych lede lys in his bedde,
Gawayn graypely at home, in gereȝ ful ryche

of hewe ;
1472   þe lady noȝt forȝate,
Com to hym to salue,
Ful erly ho watȝ hym ate,
His mode for to remwe.

XIV.

1476 Ho commes to þe cortyn, & at þe knyȝt totes,
& Wawen her welcumed worþy on fyrst,

& ho hym ȝeldeȝ aȝayn, ful ȝerne of hir wordeȝ,
Setteȝ hir sof[t]ly by his syde, & swyþely ho laȝeȝ,

1480 & wyth a luflych loke ho layde² hym þese wordeȝ :
" Syr, ȝif ȝe be Wawen, wonder me þynkkeȝ,
Wyȝe þat is so wel wrast alway to god,
& conneȝ not of compaynye þe costeȝ vnder-take,

1484 & if mon kennes yow hom to knowe, ȝe kest hom of

your mynde ;

þou hatȝ for-ȝeten ȝederly þat ȝisterday I taȝtte
Bi alder-truest token of talk þat I cowþe."
" What is þat ? " quoth þe wyghe, " I-wysse I wot neuer,
1488 If hit be sothe þat ȝe breue, þe blame is myn awen."

---

¹ The MS. is here almost illegible.   ² sayde (?).

"I taught you of kissing," she says, "that becomes every knight."

"ӡet I kende yow of kyssyng," q*uoth* þe clere þenne,

"Quere-so countenaunce is couþe, quikly to clayme,

þat bicumes vche a knyӡt, þat cortaysy vses."

1492 "Do way," q*uoth* þat derf mon, "my dere, þat speche,

Gawayne says that he must not take that which is forbidden.

For þat durst I not do, lest I denayed were,

If I were werned, I were wrang I-wysse, ӡif I profered."

"Ma fay," q*uoth* þe mere wyf, "ӡe may not be werned,

He is told that he is strong enough to enforce it.

1496 ӡe ar stif in-noghe to constrayne wyth strenkþe, ӡif yow lykeӡ,

ӡif any were so vilanous þat yow denaye[1] wolde."

"ӡe, be god," q*uoth* Gawayn, "good is your speche,

Bot þrete is vn-þryuande in þede þer I lende,

The knight replies that every gift is worthless that is not given willingly.

1500 & vche gift þat is geuen not with goud wylle;

I am at your comaundement, to kysse quen yow lykeӡ,

ӡe may lach quen yow lyst, & leue quen yow þynkkeӡ, in space."

The lady stoops down and kisses him.

1504 þe lady louteӡ a-doun,

& comlyly kysses his face,

Much speche þay þer expoun,

Of druryes greme & grace.

XV.

"I would learn," she says, "why you, who are so young and active,

1508 "I woled[2] wyt at yow, wyӡe," þat worþy þer sayde,

"& yow wrathed not þer-wyth, what were þe skylle,

þat so ӡong & so ӡepe, as ӡe [ar] at þis tyme,

So cortayse, so knyӡtyly, as ӡe ar knowen oute,

so skilled in the true sport of love,

1512 & of alle cheualry to chose, þe chef þyng a-losed,

Is[3] þe lel layk of luf, þe lettrure of armes;

For to telle of þis tenelyng of, þis trwe knyӡteӡ,

Hit is þe tytelet, token, & tyxt of her werkkeӡ,

1516 How le[des] for her lele luf hor lyueӡ han auntered,

Endured for her drury dulful stoundeӡ,

& after wenged with her walour & voyded her care,

and so renowned a knight,

& broӡt blysse in-to boure, with bountees hor awen.

1520 & ӡe ar knyӡt comlokest kyd of your elde,

---

[1] de vaye, in MS.   [2] wolde (?).   [3] In (?).

Your wordę & your worchip walkeȝ ay quere,   [Fol. 111b.]

& I haf seten by your-self here sere twyes,

ȝet herde I neuer of your hed helde no wordeȝ   havenever talked to me of love.

1524 þat euer longed to luf, lasse ne more;

& ȝe, þat ar so cortays & coynt of your hetes,

Oghe to a ȝonke þynk ȝern to schewe,   You ought to show a young thing like me some token of 'true-love's crafts.'

& teche sum tokeneȝ of trweluf craftes.

1528 Why ar ȝe lewed, þat alle þe los ȝweldeȝ,

Oþer elles ȝe demen me to dille, your dalyaunce to herken?

        for schame!

        I com hider sengel, & sitte,

1532   To lerne at yow sum game,

        Dos, techeȝ me of your wytte,   So teach me of your 'wit' while my lord is from home."

        Whil my lorde is fro hame."

XVI.

"In goud fayþe," quoth Gawayn, "god yow for-ȝelde,   "It is a great pleasure to me," says Sir Gawayne, "to hear you talk,

1536 Gret is þe gode gle, & gomen to me huge,

þat so worþy as ȝe wolde wynne hidere,

& pyne yow with so pouer a mon, as play wyth your knyȝt,

With any skynneȝ countenaunce, hit keuereȝ me ese;

1540 Bot to take þe toruayle¹ to my-self, to trwluf expoun,   but I cannot undertake the task to expound true-love and tales of arms.

& towche þe temeȝ of tyxt, & taleȝ of armeȝ,

To yow þat, I wot wel, weldeȝ more slyȝt

Of þat art, bi þe half, or a hundreth of seche

1544 As I am, oþer euer schal, in erde þer I leue,

Hit were a fole fele-folde, my fre, by my trawþe.

I wolde yowre wylnyng worche at my myȝt,   I will, however, act according to your will,

As I am hyȝly bihalden, & euer-more wylle

1548 Be seruaunt to your-seluen, so saue me dryȝtyn!"   and ever be your servant."

þus hym frayned þat fre, & fondet hym ofte,

For to haf wonnen hym to woȝe, what-so scho þoȝt elleȝ,

Bot he defended hym so fayr, þat no faut semed,   Thus Gawayne defends himself.

1552 Ne non euel on nawþer halue, nawþer þay wysten,

        bot blysse;

        ¹ tornayle (?).

4

þay laȝed & layked longe,
At þe last scho con hym kysse,

The lady, having kissed the knight, takes leave of him. 1556 Hir leue fayre con scho fonge,
& went hir waye I-wysse.

XVII.

Gawayne rises, hears mass, and then dines.
[Fol. 112.] Then ruþes hym þe renk, & ryses to þe masse,
& siþen hor diner watȝ dyȝt & derely serued.

Meanwhile the lord pursues the wild boar, 1560 þe lede with þe ladyeȝ layked alle day,
Bot þe lorde ouer þe londeȝ launced ful ofte,
Sweȝ his vncely swyn, þat swyngeȝ bi þe bonkkeȝ,

that bit the backs of his hounds asunder, & bote þe best of his bracheȝ þe bakkeȝ in sunder;
1564 þer he bode in his bay, tel[1] bawe-men hit breken,
& made[2] hym, maw-gref his hed, for to mwe vtter;

and caused the stiffest of the hunters to start. So felle floneȝ þer flete, when þe folk gedered;
Bot ȝet þe styffest to start bi stoundeȝ he made,
1568 Til at þe last he watȝ so mat, he myȝt no more renne,

The boar runs into a hole in a rock by the side of a brook. Bot in þe hast þat he myȝt, he to a hole wynneȝ,
Of a rasse, bi a rokk, þer renneȝ þe borrne,
He gete þe bonk at his bak, bigyneȝ to scrape,

The froth foams at his mouth. 1572 þe froþe femed[3] at his mouth vnfayre bi þe wykeȝ,
Whetteȝ his whyte tuscheȝ; with hym þen irked
Alle þe burneȝ so bolde, þat hym by stoden,

None durst approach him, To nye hym on-ferum, bot neȝe hym non durst
1576   for woþe;
He hade hurt so mony byforne,
þat al þuȝt[4] þenne ful loþe,

so many had he torn with his tusks. Be more wyth his tuscheȝ torne,
1580 þat breme watȝ [&] brayn-wod botheȝ.

XVIII.

The knight, seeing the boar at bay, Til þe knyȝt com hym-self, kachande his blonk,
Syȝ hym byde at þe bay, his burneȝ bysyde,
alights from his horse, He lyȝtes luflych adoun, leueȝ, his corsour,

[1] til (?)   [2] madee, in MS.   [3] fomed (?).   [4] þoȝt (?).

1584 Braydeȝ out a bryȝt bront, & bigly forth strydeȝ,
Foundeȝ fast þurȝ þe forth, þer þe felle bydeȝ,
þe wylde watȝ war of þe wyȝe with weppen in honde,
Hef hyȝly þe here, so hetterly he fnast,

and seeks to attack him with his sword.

1588 þat fele ferde for þe frekeȝ,[1] lest felle hym þe worre;
þe swyn setteȝ hym out on þe segge euen,
þat þe burne & þe bor were boþe vpon hepeȝ,
In þe wyȝt-est[2] of þe water, þe worre had þat oþer;

The "swine sets out" upon the man,

1592 For þe mon merkkeȝ hym wel, as þay mette fyrst,
Set sadly þe scharp in þe slot euen,
Hit hym vp to þe hult, þat þe hert schyndered,
& he ȝarrande hym ȝelde, & ȝedoun[3] þe water,
1596   ful tyt;

who, aiming well,

wounds him in the pit of the stomach.

A hundreth houndeȝ hym hent,
þat bremely con hym bite,
Burneȝ him broȝt to bent,
1600   & doggeȝ to dethe endite.

[Fol. 112b.]
The boar is soon bitten to death by a hundred hounds.

XIX.

There watȝ blawyng of prys in mony breme horne,
Heȝe halowing on hiȝe, with haþeleȝ þat myȝt;
Brachetes bayed þat best, as bidden þe maystereȝ,
1604 Of þat chargeaunt chace þat were chef hunteȝ.

Then was there blowing of horns,

and baying of hounds.

þenne a wyȝe þat watȝ wys vpon wod crafteȝ,
To vnlace þis bor lufly bigynneȝ;
Fyrst he heweȝ of his hed, & on hiȝe setteȝ,
1608 & syþen rendeȝ him al roghe bi þe rygge after,
Braydeȝ out þe boweles, brenneȝ hom on glede,
With bred blent þer-with his braches rewardeȝ;
Syþen he britneȝ out þe brawen in bryȝt brode [s]cheldeȝ,
1612 & hatȝ out þe hastletteȝ, as hiȝtly bisemeȝ,
& ȝet hem halcheȝ al hole þe halueȝ to-geder,
& syþen on a stif stange stoutly hem hengeȝ.

One wise in woodcraft begins to unlace the boar.

First he hews off the head, then rends him by the back.

He next removes the bowels, broils them on the ashes, and therewith rewards his hounds.

Then the hastlets are removed. The two halves are next bound together and hung upon a pole.

---

[1] freke (?).   [2] wyȝcrest (?); this word is doubtful in the MS.
[3] ȝede doun (?).

Now with þis ilk swyn þay swengen to home;

1616 Þe bores hed watȝ borne bifore þe burnes seluen,

Þat him for-ferde in þe forþe, þurȝ forse of his honde,

so stronge;

Til he seȝ syr Gawayne,

1620 In halle hym þoȝt ful longe,

He calde, & he com gayn,

His feeȝ þer for to fonge.

XX.

Þe lorde ful lowde with lote, & laȝed myry,

1624 When he seȝe syr G: with solace he spekeȝ;

Þe goude ladyeȝ were geten, & gedered þe meyny,

He scheweȝ hem þe scheldeȝ, & schapes hem þe tale,

Of þe largesse, & þe lenþe, þe liþerneȝ alse,

1628 Of þe were of þe wylde swyn, in wod þer he fled.

Þat oþer knyȝt ful comly comended his dedeȝ,

& praysed hit as gret prys, þat he proued hade;

For suche a brawne of a best, þe bolde burne sayde,

1632 Ne such sydes of a swyn, segh he neuer are.

Þenne hondeled þay þe hoge hed, þe hende mon hit

praysed,

& let lodly þerat þe lorde forto here:

"Now Gawayn," quoth þe god mon, "þis gomen is

your awen,

1636 Bi fyn forwarde & faste, faythely ȝe knowe,

"Hit is sothe," quoth þe segge, "& as siker trwe;

Alle my get I schal yow gif agayn, bi my trawþe."

He [hent] þe haþel aboute þe halse, & hendely hym

kysses,

1640 & efter-sones of þe same he serued hym þere.

"Now ar we euen," quoth þe haþel, "in þis euen-tide,

Of alle þe couenauntes þat we knyt, syþen I com hider,

bi lawe;"

1644 Þe lorde sayde, "bi saynt Gile,

Ȝe ar þe best þat I knowe,

ȝe ben ryche in a whyle,
Such chaffer & ȝe drowe."

XXI.

1648 Þenne þay teldet tableȝ [on] trestes alofte,

Tables are raised aloft,

Kesten cloþeȝ vpon, clere lyȝt þenne

cloths cast upon them,

Wakned bi woȝeȝ, waxen torches

and torches are lighted.

Seggeȝ sette, & serued in sale al aboute;
1652 Much glam & gle glent vp þer-inne,

With much mirth and glee,

Aboute þe fyre vpon flet, & on fele wyse,
At þe soper & after, mony aþel songeȝ,

supper is served in the hall,

As coundutes of kryst-masse, & caroleȝ newe,
1656 With alle þe manerly merþe þat mon may of telle.
& euer oure luflych knyȝt þe lady bi-syde;

and ever our lovely knight by the lady sits,

Such semblaunt to þat segge semly ho made,
Wyth stille stollen countenaunce, þat stalworth to plese,

who does all she can to please her companion.

1660 Þat al for-wondered watȝ þe wyȝe, & wroth with hym-
seluen,
Bot he nolde not for his nurture nurne hir a-ȝayneȝ,
Bot dalt with hir al in daynte, how-se-euer þe dede turned
to wrast;
1664 Quen þay hade played in halle,

When they had long played in the hall,

As lange as hor wylle hom last,
To chambre he¹ con hym calle,

they proceeded "to chamber."

& to þe chemne þay past.

XXII.

1668 Ande þer þay dronken, & dalten, & demed eft nwe,

There they drank and discoursed.

To norne on þe same note, on nweȝereȝ euen;
Bot þe knyȝt craued leue to kayre on þe morn,

Gawayne begs leave to depart on the morrow.

For hit watȝ neȝ at þe terme, þat he to² schulde.
1672 Þe lorde hym letted of þat, to lenge hym resteyed,

[Fol. 113b.]

& sayde, "as I am trwe segge, I siker my trawþe,

His host swears to him,

Þou schal cheue to þe grene chapel, þy charres to make,

that he shall come to the Green

¹ ho (?).　　² te (?).

Leude, on nwȝereȝ lyȝt, longe bifore pryme ;

1676 For-þy þow lye in þy loft, & lach þyn ese,

& I schal hunt in þis holt, & halde þe towcheȝ,

Chaunge wyth þe cheuisaunce, bi þat I charre hider;

For I haf fraysted þe twys, & faythful I fynde þe,

1680 Now þrid tyme þrowe best þenk on þe morne,

Make we mery quyl we may, & mynne vpon Ioye,

For þe lur may mon lach, when so mon lykeȝ."

Þis watȝ grayþely graunted, & Gawayn is lenged,

1684 Bliþe broȝt watȝ hym drynk, & þay to bedde ȝeden,

with liȝt ;

Syr G : lis & slepes,

Ful stille & softe al niȝt ;

1688 Þe lorde þat his crafteȝ kepes,

Ful erly he watȝ diȝt.

XXIII.

After messe a morsel he & his men token,

Miry watȝ þe mornyng, his mounture he askes ;

1692 Alle þe haþeles þat on horse schulde helden hym after,

Were boun busked on hor blonkkeȝ, bi-fore[1] þe halle ȝateȝ ;

Ferly fayre watȝ þe folde, for þe forst clenged,

In rede rudede vpon rak rises þe sunne,

1696 & ful clere costeȝ[2] þe clowdes of þe welkyn.

Hunteres vnhardeled bi a holt syde,

Rocheres roungen bi rys, for rurde of her hornes ;

Summe fel in þe fute, þer þe fox bade,

1700 Trayleȝ ofte a trayteres,[3] bi traunt of her wyles ;

A kenet kryes þerof, þe hunt on hym calles,

His felaȝes fallen hym to, þat fnasted ful þike,

Runnen forth in a rabel, in his ryȝt fare ;

1704 & he fyskeȝ hem by-fore, þay founden hym sone,

& quen þay seghe hym with syȝt, þay sued hym fast,

Wreȝande hym ful weterly with a wroth noyse ;

[1] bi-forere, in MS.   [2] casteȝ (?).   [3] trayveres (?).

& he trantes & tornayeȝ þurȝ mony tene greue ;

1708 Hamlouneȝ, & herkeneȝ, bi heggeȝ ful ofte ;

At þo last bi a littel dich he lepeȝ ouer a spenné,

Steleȝ out ful stilly bi a strothe rande,

Went haf wylt of þe wode, with wyleȝ fro þe houndes,

1712 þenne watȝ he went, er he wyst, to¹ a wale tryster,

þer þre þro at a þrich þat hym at ones,

al graye ;

He blenched aȝayn bilyue,

1716 & stifly start on-stray,

With alle þe wo on lyue,

To þe wod he went away.

and pursue him through many a rough grove.

[Fol. 114.] The fox aȝ last leaps over a spinny, and by a rugged path seeks to get clear from the hounds. He comes upon one of the hunting stations, where he is attacked by the dogs. However, he slips them,

and makes again for the wood.

XXIV.

Thenne watȝ hit lif vpon list to lyþen þe houndeȝ,

1720 When alle þe mute hade hym met, menged to-geder,

Suche a sorȝe at þat syȝt þay sette on his hede,

As alle þe clamberande clyffes hade clatered on hepes ;

Here he watȝ halawed, when haþeleȝ hym metten,

1724 Loude he watȝ ȝayned, with ȝarande speche ;

þer he watȝ þreted, & ofte þef called,

& ay þe titleres at his tayl, þat tary he ne myȝt ;

Ofte he watȝ runnen at, when he out rayked,

1728 & ofte reled in aȝayn, so reniarde watȝ wylé.

& ȝe he lad hem bi lag, mon, þe lorde & his meyny ;

On þis maner bi þe mounted, quyle myd, ouer, vnder,

Whyle þe hende knyȝt at home holsumly slepeȝ,

1732 With-inne þe comly cortynes, on þe colde morne

Bot þe lady for luf let not to slepe,

Ne þe purpose to payre, þat pyȝt in hir hert,

Bot ros hir vp radly, rayked hir þeder,

1736 In a mery mantyle, mete to þe erþe,

þat watȝ furred ful fyne with felleȝ, wel pured,

No hweȝ goud on hir hede, bot þe haȝer stones

Then was it fine sport to listen to the hounds,

and the hallooing of the hunters.

There the fox was threatened and called a thief.

But Reynard was wily, and led them astray over mounts. Meanwhile the knight at home soundly sleeps within his comely curtains.

The lady of the castle, clothed in a rich mantle,

¹ to to, in MS.

Trased aboute hir tressoʋr, be twenty in clusteres;

her throat and bosom all bare,
1740 Hir þryuen face & hir þrote þrowen al naked,

Hir brest bare bifore, & bihinde eke.

comes to Gawayne's chamber,
Ho comeȝ with-inne þe chambre dore, & closes hit hir
     after,

opens a window, and says,
Wayneȝ[1] vp a wyndow, & on þe wyȝe calleȝ,

1744 & radly þus rehayted hym, with hir riche wordeȝ,
      with[2] chere;

"Ah! man, how
   "A! mon, how may þou slepe,

[Fol. 114b.]
   þis morning is so clere?"

canst thou sleep, this morning is so clear?"
1748 He watȝ in drówping depe,

   Bot þenne he con hir here.

XXV.

The knight was then dreaming of his forthcoming adventure at the Green Chapel.
In dreȝ droupyng of dreme draueled þat noble,

As mon þat watȝ in mornyng of mony þro þoȝtes,

1752 How þat destiné schulde þat day [dyȝt] his wyrde,

At þe grene chapel, when he þe gome metes,

& bi-houes his buffet abide, with-oute debate more;

He awakes and speaks to his fair visitor,
Bot quen þat comly he keuered his wyttes,

1756 Swenges out of þe sweuenes, & swareȝ with hast.

þe lady luflych com laȝande swete,

who sweetly kisses him.
Felle ouer his fayre face, & fetly hym kyssed;

He welcumeȝ hir worþily, with a wale chere;

1760 He seȝ hir so glorious, & gayly atyred,

So fautles of hir fetures, & of so fyne hewes,

Great joy warms the heart of Sir Gawayne,
Wiȝt wallande Ioye warmed his hert;

With smoþe smylyng & smolt þay smeten in-to merþe,

1764 þat al watȝ blis & bonchef, þat breke hem bi-twene,
     & wynne;

þay lanced wordes gode,

Much wele þen watȝ þer-inne,

and "great peril between them stood."
1768 Gret perile bi-twene hem stod,

Nif mare of hir knyȝt mynne.

XXVI.

For þat prynce of pris depresed hym so þikke,

Nurned hym so neȝe þe þred, þat nede hym bi-houed,

1772 Oþer lach þer hir luf, oþer lodly refuse ;

He cared for his cortaysye, lest craþayn he were,

& more for his meschef, ȝif he schulde make synne,

& be traytor to þat tolke, þat þat telde aȝt.

1776 "God schylde," quoth þe schalk, "þat schal not be-

falle!"

Wíth luf-laȝyng a lyt, he layd hym by-syde

Alle þe specheȝ of specialté þat sprange of her mouthe.

Quoth þat burde to þe burne, "blame ȝe disserue,

1780 Ȝif ȝe luf not þat lyf þat ȝe lye nexte,

Bifore alle þe wyȝeȝ in þe worlde, wounded in hert,

Bot if ȝe haf a lemman, a leuer, þat yow lykeȝ better,

& folden fayth to þat fre, festned so harde,

1784 þat yow lausen ne lyst, & þat I leue nouþe ;

And þat ȝe telle me þat, now trwly I pray yow,

For alle þe lufeȝ vpon lyue, layne not þe soþe,

for gile."

1788   þe knyȝt sayde, "be sayn Ion,"

& smeþely con he smyle,

"In fayth I welde riȝt non,

Ne non wil welde þe quile."

The knight is
sorely pressed.

He fears lest he
should become a
traitor to his
host.

The lady inquires
whether he has a
mistress that he
loves better than
her.

[Fol. 115.]

Sir Gawayne
swears by St.
John that he
neither has nor
desires one.

XXVII.

1792 "þat is a worde," quoth þat wyȝt, "þat worst is of alle,

Bot I am swared for soþeȝ þat sore me þinkkeȝ ;

Kysse me now comly, & I schal cach heþen,

I may bot mourne vpon molde, as may þat much louyes."

1796 Sykande ho sweȝe doun, & semly hym kyssed,

& siþen ho seueres hym fro, & says as ho stondes,

"Now, dere, at þis de-partyng, do me þis ese,

Gif me sumquat of þy gifte, þi gloue if[1] hit were,

1800 þat I may mynne on þe mon, my mournyng to lassen."

She then kisses
him, sighing for
sorrow.

She desires some
gift,
by which to re-
member him.

[1] of, in MS.

"Now I-wysse," quoth þat wyʒe, "I wolde I hade here
þe leuest þing for þy luf, þat I in londe welde,

Gawayne tells her that she is worthy of a better gift than he can bestow.
1804 For ʒe haf deserued, forsoþe, sellyly ofte
More rewarde bi resoun, þen I reche myʒt,
Bot to dele yow for drurye, þat dawed bot neked;
Hit is not your honour to haf at þis tyme
A gloue for a garysoun, of Gawayneʒ gifteʒ,

He has no men with mails containing precious things.
1808 & I am here [on] an erande in erdeʒ vncouþe,
& haue no men wyth no maleʒ, with menskful þingeʒ
þat mislykeʒ me, ladé, for luf at þis tyme,[1]
Iche tolke mon do as he is tan, tas to non ille,

Then says that lovesome,
1812 ne pine,"
"Nay, hende of hyʒe honours,"

"Though I had nought of yours, yet should ye have of mine."
Quoth þat lufsum vnder lyne,
"Þaʒ I hade oʒt[2] of youreʒ,
1816 ʒet schulde ʒe haue of myne."

XXVIII.

She offers him a gold ring,
Ho raʒt hym a riche rynk[3] of red golde werkeʒ,
Wyth a starande ston, stondande alofte,
þat bere blusschande bemeʒ as þe bryʒt sunne;
1820 Wyt ʒe wel, hit watʒ worth wele ful hoge.

but he refuses to accept it, [Fol. 115b.] as he has none to give in return.
Bot þe renk hit renayed, & redyly he sayde,
"I wil no gifteʒ for gode, my gay, at þis tyme;
I haf none yow to norne, ne noʒt wyl I take."
1824 Ho bede hit hym ful bysily, & he hir bode wernes,
& swere swyftel[y] his sothe, þat he hit sese nolde;

Very sorrowful was that fair one on account of his refusal.
& ho sore þat he forsoke, & sayde þer-after,
"If ʒe renay my rynk,[3] to ryche for hit semeʒ,
1828 ʒe wolde not so hyʒly halden be to me,
I schal gif yow my girdel, þat gayneʒ yow lasse."
Ho laʒt a lace lyʒtly, þat[4] leke vmbe hir syde,

She takes off her "girdle,"
Knit vpon hir kyrtel, vnder þe clere mantyle,
1832 Gered hit watʒ with grene sylke, & with golde schaped,

---

[1] tyne, in MS.　　[2] noʒt (?).　　[3] ryng (?).　　[4] þat þat, in MS.

Noȝt bot arounde brayden, beten with fyngreȝ;
& þat ho bede to þe burne, & blyþely bi-soȝt

Þaȝ hit vn-worþi were, þat he hit take wolde.

1836 & he nay þat he nolde neghe in no wyse,
Nauþer golde ne garysoun, er god hym grace sende,
To acheue to þe chaunce þat he hade chosen þere.

" & þerfore, I pray yow, displese yow noȝt,

1840 & letteȝ be your bisinesse, for I bayþe hit yow neuer
to graunte ;
I am derely to yow biholde,
Bi-cause of your sembelaunt,

1844 & euer in hot & colde
To be your trwe seruaunt."

XXIX.

" Now forsake ȝe þis silke," sayde þe burde þenne,
" For hit is symple in hit-self, & so hit wel semeȝ ?

1848 Lo ! so hit is littel, & lasse hit is worþy ;
Bot who-so knew þe costes þat knit ar þer-inne,
He wolde hit prayse at more prys, parauenture ;

For quat gome so is gorde with þis grene lace,

1852 While he hit hade hemely halched aboute,

Þer is no haþel vnder heuen to-hewe hym þat myȝt ;
For he myȝt not be slayn, for slyȝt vpon erþe."

Þen kest þe knyȝt, & hit come to his hert,

1856 Hit were a Iuel for þe Iopardé, þat hym iugged were,
When he acheued to þe chapel, his chek forto fech ;
Myȝ¹ he haf slypped to be vn-slayn, þe sleȝt were noble.

Þenne he þulged with hir þrepe, & þoled hir to speke,

1860 & ho bere on hym þe belt, & bede hit hym swyþe,
& he grauted, & [ho] hym gafe with a goud wylle,
& bi-soȝt hym, for hir sake, discouer hit neuer,

Bot to lelly layne for² hir lorde ; þe leude hym acordeȝ,

1864 Þat neuer wyȝe schulde hit wyt, I-wysse, bot þay twayne,
for noȝte ;

¹ myȝt (?).   ² fro (?).

He þonkked hir oft ful swyþe,
Ful þro with hert & þoȝt.

By that time the
lady has kissed
him thrice. 1868 Bi þat on þrynne syþe,
Ho hatȝ kyst þe knyȝt so toȝt.

XXX.

Then she takes
her leave. Thenne lachcheȝ ho hir leue, & leueȝ hym þere,
For more myrþe of þat mon moȝt hŏ not gete;
Gawayne then
dresses himself, 1872 When ho[1] watȝ gon, syr G. gereȝ hym sone,
Rises, & riches hym in araye noble,
and conceals the
love-lace about
his person. Lays vp þe luf-lace, þe lady hym raȝt,
Hid hit ful holdely, þer he hit eft fonde;
1876 Syþen cleuely to þe chapel choses he þe waye,
He then hies to
mass, Preuely aproched to a prest, & prayed hym þere
þat he wolde lyfte[2] his lyf, & lern hym better,
How his sawle schulde be saued, when he schuld
seye heþen.
and shrives him
of his misdeeds, 1880 Þere he schrof hym schyrly, & schewed his mysdedeȝ,
Of þe more & þe mynne, & merci besecheȝ,
and prays for ab-
solution. & of absolucioun he on þe segge calles;
& he asoyled hym surely, & sette hym so clene,
He returns to the
hall, and makes
himself so merry
among the ladies, 1884 As domeȝ-day schulde haf ben diȝt on þe morn.
& syþen he mace hym as mery among þe fre ladyes,
with comely
carols, With comlych caroles, & alle kynnes ioye,
As neuer he did bot þat daye, to þe derk nyȝt,
1888 with blys;
Vche mon hade daynte þare,
that they said, Of hym, & sayde I-wysse,
"Thus merry
was he never be-
fore since hither
he came." 1892 Þus myry he watȝ neuer are,
Syn he com hider, er þis.

XXXI.

Gawayne's host is
still in the field. Now hym lenge in þat lee, þer luf hym bi-tyde;
Ȝet is þe lorde on þe launde, ledande his gomnes,

[1] he, in MS.   [2] lyste (?).

He haꝫ forfaren þis fox, þat he folꝫed longe ;

1896 As he sprent ouer a spenné, to spye þe schrewe,

þer as he herd þe howndes, þat hasted hym swyþe,

Renaud com richchande þurꝫ a roꝫe greue,

& alle þe rabel in a res, ryꝫt at his heleꝫ.

1900 þe wyꝫe watꝫ war of þe wylde, & warly abides,

& braydeꝫ out þe bryꝫt bronde, & at þe best casteꝫ ;

& he schunt for þe scharp, & schulde haf arered,

A rach rapes hym to, ryꝫt er he myꝫt,

1904 & ryꝫt bifore þe hors fete þay fel on hym alle,

& woried me þis wyly wyth a wroth noyse.

þe lorde lyꝫteꝫ bi-lyue, & cacheꝫ by¹ sone,

Rased hym ful radly out of þe rach mouþes,

1908 Haldeꝫ heꝫe ouer his hede, haloweꝫ faste,

& þer bayen hym mony bray² houndeꝫ ;

Huntes hyꝫed hem þeder, with horneꝫ ful mony,

Ay rechatande aryꝫt til þay þe renk seꝫen ;

1912 Bi þat watꝫ comen his compeyny noble,

Alle þat euer ber bugle blowed at ones,

& alle þise oþer halowed, þat hade no hornes,

Hit watꝫ þe myriest mute þat euer men herde,

1916 þe rich rurd þat þer watꝫ raysed for renaude saule,

with lote ;

Hor houndeꝫ þay þer rewarde,

Her³ hedeꝫ þay fawne & frote,

1920 & syþen þay tan reynarde,

& tyrnen of his cote.

XXXII.

& þenne þay helden to home, for hit watꝫ nieꝫ nyꝫt,

Strakande ful stoutly in hor store horneꝫ ;

1924 þe lorde is lyꝫt at þe laste at hys lef home,

Fyndeꝫ fire vpon flet, þe freke þer by-side,

Sir Gawayn þe gode, þat glad watꝫ with alle,

Among þe ladies for luf he ladde much ioye,

Side notes:
He has destroyed the fox.
[Fol. 116b.] He spied Reynard coming through a "rough grove,"
and tried to hit him with his sword.
The fox "shunts" and is seized by one of the dogs.
The lord takes him out of the hound's mouth.
Hunters hasten thither with horns full many.
It was the merriest meet that ever was heard.
The hounds are rewarded,
and then they take Reynard and "turn off his coat."
The hunters then hasten home.
The lord at last alights at his dear home,
where he finds Gawayne amusing the ladies.

¹ hym (?).   ² braþ (?).   ³ Her her, in MS.

1928 He were a bleaunt of blwe, þat bradde to þe erþe,
      His surkot semed hym wel, þat softe watȝ forred,
      & his hode of þat ilke henged on his schulder,

The knight comes forward and welcomes his host,

      Blande al of blaunner were boþe al aboute.
1932 He meteȝ me þis god man in myddeȝ þe flore,
      & al with gomen he hym gret, & goudly he sayde,
      "I schal fylle vpon fyrst oure forwardeȝ nouþe,

[Fol. 117.] and according to covenant kisses him thrice. (See l. 1868.)

      þat we spedly han spoken, þer spared watȝ no drynk;"
1936 þen acoles he [þe] knyȝt, & kysses hym þryes,
      As sauerly & sadly as he hem sette couþe.

"By Christ," says the other, "ye have had much bliss!"

      "Bi kryst," quoth þat oþer knyȝt, "ȝe cach much sele,
      In cheuisaunce of þis chaffer, ȝif ȝe hade goud chepeȝ."
1940 "ȝe of þe chepe no charg," quoth chefly þat oþer,
      "As is pertly payed þe chepeȝ þat I aȝte."
      "Mary," quoth þat oþer mon, "myn is bi-hynde,

I have hunted all day and have gotten nothing, but the skin of this foul fox,

      For I haf hunted al þis day, & noȝt haf I geten,
1944 Bot þis foule fox felle, þe fende haf þe godeȝ,
      & þat is ful pore, for to pay for suche prys þinges,

a poor reward for three such kisses."

      As ȝe haf þryȝt me here, þro suche þre cosses,
      so gode."
1948   "Inoȝ," quoth syr Gawayn,
       "I þonk yow, bi þe rode;"

He then tells him how the fox was slain.

      & how þe fox watȝ slayn,
      He tolde hym, as þay stode.

XXXIII.

With much mirth and minstrelsy they made merry,

1952 With merþe & mynstralsye, wyth meteȝ at hor wylle,
      þay maden as mery as any men moȝten,
      With laȝyng of ladies, with loteȝ of bordeȝ;
      Gawayn & þe gode mon so glad were þay boþe,
1956 Bot if þe douthe had doted, oþer dronken ben oþer,
      Boþe þe mon & þe meyny maden mony iapeȝ,

until the time came for them to part.

      Til þe sesoun watȝ seȝen, þat þay seuer moste;
      Burneȝ to hor bedde be-houed at þe laste.
1960 þenne loȝly his leue at þe lorde fyrst

Gawayne takes leave of his host,

      Fochcheȝ þis fre mon, & fayre he hym þonkkeȝ;

"Of such a sellyly¹ soiorne, as I haf hade here,

Your honour, at þis hyȝe fest, þe hyȝe kyng yow ȝelde!

and thanks him for his happy "sojourn."

1964 I ȝef yow me for on of youreȝ, if yowre-self lykeȝ,

For I mot nedes, as ȝe wot, meue to morne;

& ȝe me take sum tolke, to teche, as ȝe hyȝt,

þe gate to þe grene chapel, as god wyl me suffer

He asks for a man to teach him the way to the Green Chapel.

1968 To dele, on nwȝereȝ day, þe dome of my wyrdes."

"In god fayþe," quoth þe god mon, "wyth a goud wylle;

Al þat euer I yow hyȝt, halde schal I rede."

Þer asyngnes he a seruaunt, to sett hym in þe waye,

A servant is assigned to him,

1972 & coundue hym by þe downeȝ, þat he no drechch had,

[Fol. 117b.]

For to f[e]rk þurȝ þe fryth, & fare at þe gaynest,

bi greue.

þe lorde Gawayn con þonk,

1976 Such worchip he wolde hym weue;

þen at þo ladyeȝ wlonk,

þe knyȝt hatȝ tan his leue.

and then he takes leave of the ladies,

XXXIV.

With care & wyth kyssyng he carppeȝ hem tille,

kissing them sorrowfully.

1980 & fele þryuande þonkkeȝ he þrat hom to haue,

& þay ȝelden hym aȝay[n] ȝeply þat ilk;

þay bikende hym to kryst, with ful colde sykyngeȝ.

They commend him to Christ.

Syþen fro þe meyny he menskly de-partes;

He then departs, thanking each one he meets "for his service and solace."

1984 Vche mon þat he mette, he made hem a þonke,

For his seruyse, & his solace, & his sere pyne,

þat þay wyth busynes had ben, aboute hym to serue;

& vche segge as sore, to seuer with hym þere,

1988 As þay hade wonde worþyly with þat wlonk euer.

þen with ledes & lyȝt he watȝ ladde to his chambre,

He retires to rest, but sleeps but little,

& blyþely broȝt to his bedde, to be at his rest;

ȝif he ne slepe soundly, say ne dar I,

¹ selly (?).

for much has he
to think of on the
morrow.

1992 For he hade muche on þe morn to mynne, ʒif he wolde,
        in poʒt ;

Let him there lie
still.

    Let hym lyʒe þere stille,
    He hatʒ[1] nere þat he soʒt,

Be still awhile
and I shall tell
how they
wrought.

1996   & ʒe wyl a whyle be stylle,
    I schal telle yow how þay wroʒt.

[FYTTE THE FOURTH.]

I.

New Year's Day
approaches,

NOW neʒeʒ þe nwʒere, & þe nyʒt passeʒ,
    þe day dryueʒ to þe derk, as dryʒtyn biddeʒ ;

The weather is
stormy.

2000 Bot wylde wedereʒ of þe worlde wakned þeroute,
    Clowdes kesten kenly þe colde to þe erþe,
    Wyth nyʒe[2] in-noghe of þe norþe, þe naked to tene ;

Snow falls,

    þe snawe snitered ful snart, þat snayped þe wylde ;

2004 þe werbelande wynde wapped fro þe hyʒe,

The dales are full
of drift.

    & drof vche dale ful of dryftes ful grete.
    þe leude lystened ful wel, þat leʒ in his bedde,
    þaʒ he lowkeʒ his liddeʒ, ful lyttel he slepes ;

Gawayne in his
bed hears each
cock that crew.
[Fol. 118.]

2008 Bi vch kok þat crue, he knwe wel þe steuen.
    Deliuerly he dressed vp, er þe day sprenged,
    For þere watʒ lyʒt of a lau[m]pe, þat lemed in his
        chambre ;

He calls for his
chamberlain,
and bids him
bring him his
armour.

    He called to his chamberlayn, þat cofly hym swared,

2012 & bede hym bryng hym his bruny, & his blonk sadel ;
    þat oþer ferkeʒ hym vp, & fecheʒ hym his wedeʒ,
    & grayþeʒ me syr Gawayn vpon a grett wyse.
    Fyrst he clad hym in his cloþeʒ, þe colde for to were ;

2016 & syþen his oþer harnays, þat holdely watʒ keped,
    Boþe his paunce, & his plateʒ, piked ful clene,

Men knock off
the rust from his
rich habergeon.

    þe ryngeʒ[3] rokked of þe roust, of his riche bruny ;
    & al watʒ fresch as vpon fyrst, & he watʒ fayn þenne

2020   to þonk ;

---

[1] watʒ (?).   [2] nywe (?).   [3] rynkeʒ (?).

He hade vpon ȝche pece,
Wypped ful wel & wlonk;
þe gayest in to Grece,
2024   þe burne bede bryng his blonk.

The knight then
calls for his steed.

II.

Whyle þe wlonkest wedes he warp on hym-seluen;
His cote, wyth þe conysaunce of þe clere werkeȝ,
Ennurned vpon veluet vertuuus[1] stoneȝ,
2028   Aboute beten, & bounden, enbrauded semeȝ,
& fayre furred with-inne wyth fayre pelures.
ȝet laft he not þe lace, þe ladieȝ gifte,
þat for-gat not Gawayn, for gode of hym-seluen;
2032   Bi he hade belted þe bronde vpon his balȝe hauncheȝ,
þenne dressed he his drurye double hym aboute;
Swyþe sweþled vmbe his swange swetely, þat knyȝt,
þe gordel of þe grene silke, þat gay wel bi-semed,
2036   Vpon þat ryol red cloþe, þat ryche watȝ to schewe.
Bot wered not þis ilk wyȝe for wele þis gordel,
For pryde of þe pendaunteȝ, þaȝ polyst þay were,
& þaȝ þe glyterande golde glent vpon endeȝ,
2040   Bot forto sauen hym-self, when suffer hym bi-houed,
To byde bale with-oute dabate, of bronde hym to were,
oþer knyffe;
Bi þat þe bolde mon boun,
2044   Wynneȝ þeroute bilyue,
Alle þe meyny of renoun,
He þonkkeȝ ofte ful ryue.

While he clothed
himself in his
rich weeds,

he forgot not
the "lace," the
lady's gift,

but with it doubly
girded his loins.

He wore it not
for its rich orna-
ments,

"but to save him-
self when it be-
hoved him to
suffer."

All the renowned
assembly he
thanks full oft.

III.

Thenne watȝ Gryngolet grayþe, þat gret watȝ & huge,
2048   & hade ben soiourned sauerly, & in a siker wyse,
Hym lyst prik for poynt, þat proude hors þenne;
þe wyȝe wynneȝ hym to, & wyteȝ on his lyre,
& sayde soberly hym-self, & by his soth swereȝ,

[Fol. 118b.]
Then was Grin-
golet arrayed,
full ready to
prick on.

[1] vertuous (?).

5

2052 "Here is a meyny in þis mote, þat on menske þenkkeȝ,

þe mon hem maynteines, ioy mot þay haue ;
þe leue lady, on lyue luf hir bityde ;
ȝif þay for charyté cherysen a gest,
2056 & halden honour in her honde, þe haþel hem ȝelde,
þat haldeȝ þe heuen vpon hyȝe, & al-so yow alle !
& ȝif I myȝt lyf vpon londe lede any quyle,
I schuld rech yow sum rewarde redyly, if I myȝt."

2060 þenne steppeȝ he in-to stirop, & strydeȝ alofte ;
His schalk schewed hym his schelde, on schulder he
        hit laȝt,
Gordeȝ to Gryngolet, with his gilt heleȝ,
& he starteȝ on þe ston, stod he no lenger,
2064   to praunce ;
His haþel on hors watȝ þenne,
þat bere his spere & launce.
" þis kastel to kryst I kenne,
2068 He gef hit ay god chaunce !"

IV.

The brygge watȝ brayde doun, & þe brode ȝateȝ
Vn-barred, & born open, vpon boþe halue ;
þe burne blessed hym bilyue, & þe bredeȝ passed ;
2072 Prayses þe porter, bifore þe prynce kneled,
Gef hym god & goud day, þat Gawayn he saue ;
& went on his way, with his wyȝe one,
þat schulde teche hym to tourne to þat tene place,
2076 þer þe ruful race he schulde re-sayue.
þay boȝen bi bonkkeȝ, þer boȝeȝ ar bare,
þay clomben bi clyffeȝ, þer clengeȝ þe colde ;
þe heuen watȝ vp halt, bot vgly þer vnder,
2080 Mist muged on þe mor, malt on þe munteȝ,
Vch hille hade a hatte, a myst-hakel huge ;
Brokeȝ byled, & breke, bi bonkkeȝ aboute,
Schyre schaterande on schoreȝ, þer þay doun schowued.
2084 Welawylle watȝ þe way, þer þay bi wod schulden,

Til hit watȝ sone sesoun, þat þe sunne ryses,
    þat tyde;
þay were on a hille ful hyȝe,

2088 þe quyte snaw lay bisyde;
þe burne þat rod hym by,
Bede his mayster abide.

until daylight.

They were then on a "hill full high."

The servant bade his master abide, saying,

V.

"For I haf wonnen yow hider, wyȝe, at þis tyme,

2092 & now nar ȝe not fer fro þat note place,
þat ȝe han spied & spuryed so specially after;
Bot I schal say yow for soþe, syþen I yow knowe,
& ȝe ar a lede vpon lyue, þat I wel louy,

2096 Wolde ȝe worch bi my wytte, ȝe worþed þe better.
þe plane þat ȝe prece to, ful perelous is halden;
þer woneȝ a wyȝe in þat waste, þe worst vpon erþe;
For he is stiffe, & sturne, & to strike louies,

2100 & more he is þen any mon vpon myddelerde,
& his body bigger þen þe best fowre,
þat ar in Arþureȝ hous, hestor[1] oþer oþer.
He cheueȝ þat chaunce at þe chapel grene;

2104 þer passes non bi þat place, so proude in his armes,
þat he ne dynneȝ hym to deþe, with dynt of his honde;
For he is a mon methles, & mercy non vses,
For be hit chorle, oþer chaplayn, þat bi þe chapel rydes,

2108 Monk, oþer masse-prest, oþer any mon elles,
Hym þynk as queme hym to quelle, as quyk go hym seluen.
For-þy I say þe as soþe as ȝe in sadel sitte,
Com ȝe þere, ȝe be kylled, [I] may þe knyȝt rede,

2112 Trawe ȝe me þat trwely, þaȝ ȝe had twenty lyues
    to spende;
He hatȝ wonyd here ful ȝore,
On bent much baret bende;

2116 Aȝayn his dynteȝ sore,
ȝe may not yow defende."

     [1] Hector (?).

"I have brought you hither.

ye are not now far from the noted place.

Full perilous is it esteemed.

The lord of that 'waste' is stiff and stern.

His body is bigger 'than the best four in Arthur's house.'

None passes by the Green Chapel, 'that he does not ding him to death with dint of his hand.'

For be it churl or chaplain, monk, mass-priest, 'or any man else,' he kills them all.

He has lived there full long.

Against his dints sore, ye may not defend you.

VI.

*Wherefore, good
Sir Gawayne, let
this man alone.*

*Go by some other
region,*

[Fol. 119b.]

*I swear by God
and all His saints,
that I will never
say that ever ye
attempted to flee
from any man."*

"For-þy, goude syr Gawayn, let þe gome one,
& gotȝ a-way sum oþer gate, vpon goddeȝ halue ;
2120 Cayreȝ bi sum oþer kyth, þer kryst mot yow spede ;
& I schal hyȝ me hom aȝayn, & hete yow fyrre,
þat I schal swere bi god, & alle his gode halȝeȝ,
As help me god & þe halydam, & oþeȝ in-noghe,
2124 þat I schal lelly yow layne, & lance neuer tale,
þat euer ȝe fondet to fle, for freke þat I wyst."

"Grant merci," quoth Gawayn, & gruchyng he sayde,
"Wel worth þe wyȝe, þat woldeȝ my gode,
2128 & þat lelly me layne, I leue wel þou woldeȝ !

*Gawayne replies
that to shun this
danger would
mark him as a
"coward knight."*

*To the Chapel,
therefore, he will
go,*

Bot helde þou it neuer so holde, & I here passed,
Founded for ferde for to fle, in fourme þat þou telleȝ,
I were a knyȝt kowarde, I myȝt not[1] be excused.
2132 Bot I wyl to þe chapel, for chaunce þat may falle,
& talk wyth þat ilk tulk þe tale þat me lyste,
Worþe hit wele, oþer wo, as þe wyrde lykeȝ
            hit hafe ;

*though the owner
thereof were a
stern knave.*

*"Full well can
God devise his
servants for to
save."*

2136   Paȝe he be a sturn knape,
        To stiȝtel, &[2] stad with staue,
        Ful wel con dryȝtyn schape,
        His seruaunteȝ forto saue."

VII.

*"Mary!" quoth
the other,
"since it pleases
thee to lose thy
life,
take thy helmet
on thy head, and
thy spear in thy
hand,
and ride down
this path by yon
rock-side,
till thou come to
the bottom of the
valley ;
Look a little to
the left,
and thou shalt
see the Chapel it-
self and the man
that guards it."*

2140 "Mary!" quoth þat oþer mon, "now þou so much spelleȝ,
þat þou wylt þyn awen nye nyme to þy-seluen,
& þe lyst lese þy lyf, þe lette I ne kepe ;
Haf here þi helme on þy hedeȝ þi spere in þi honde,
2144 & ryde me doun þis ilk rake, bi ȝon rokke syde,
Til þou be broȝt to þe boþem of þe brem valay ;
Penne loke a littel on þe launde, on þi lyfte honde,
& þou schal se in þat slade þe self chapel,
2148 & þe borelych burne on bent, þat hit kepeȝ.
Now fareȝ wel on godeȝ half, Gawayn þe noble,

---

[1] mot, in MS.   [2] & &, in MS.

For alle þe golde vpon grounde I nolde go wyth þe,
Ne bere þe felaȝschip þurȝ þis fryth on fote fyrre."

2152 Bi þat þe wyȝe in þe wod wendeȝ his brydel,
Hit þe hors with þe heleȝ, as harde ás he myȝt,
Lepeȝ hym ouer þe launde, & leueȝ þe knyȝt þere,
al one.

Having thus spoken, the guide takes leave of the knight.

2156   " Bi goddeȝ self," quoth Gawayn,
    " I wyl nauþer grete ne grone,
    To goddeȝ wylle I am ful bayn,
    & to hym I haf me tone."

"By·God's self," says Sir Gawayne, "I will neither weep nor groan.
To God's will I am full ready."

VIII.

2160 Thenne gyrdeȝ he to Gryngolet, & gedereȝ þe rake,
Schowueȝ in bi a schore, at a schaȝe syde,
Rideȝ þurȝ þe roȝe bonk, ryȝt to þe dale; •
& þenne he wayted hym aboute, & wylde hit hym þoȝt,

[Fol. 120.]
Then he pursues his journey,

rides through the dale, and looks about.

2164 & seȝe no syngne of resette, bi-sydeȝ nowhere,
Bot hyȝe bonkkeȝ & brent, vpon boþe halue,
& ruȝe knokled knarreȝ, with knorned stoneȝ;
þe skweȝ of þe scowtes skayued¹ hym þoȝt.

He sees no sign of a resting-place, but only high and steep banks.

2168 þenne he houed, & wyth-hylde his hors at þat tyde,
& ofte chaunged his cher, þe chapel to seche;
He seȝ non suche in no syde, & selly hym þoȝt,
Sone a lyttel on a launde, a lawe as hit we[re];

No chapel could he discern.

2172 A balȝ berȝ, bi a bonke, þe brymme by-syde,
Bi a forȝ of a flode, þat ferked þare;
þe borne blubred þer-inne, as hit boyled hade.
þe knyȝt kacheȝ his caple, & com to þe lawe,

At last he sees a hill by the side of a stream;

Thither he goes,

2176 Liȝteȝ doun luflyly, & at a lynde tacheȝ
þe rayne, & his riche, with a roȝe braunche;
þenne he boȝeȝ to þe berȝe, aboute hit he walkeȝ,
Debetande with hym-self, quat hit be myȝt.

alights and fastens his horse to a branch of a tree.

He walks around the hill, debating with himself what it might be,

2180 Hit hade a hole on þe ende, & on ayþer syde,
& ouer-growen with gresse in glodes ay where,
& al watȝ holȝ in-with, no-bot an olde caue,

¹ skayned (?).

and at last finds an old cave in the crag.	Or a creuisse of an olde cragge, he couþe hit noȝt deme
2184	with spelle,
	" We,¹ lorde," quoth þe gentyle knyȝt,
	" Wheþer þis be þe grene chapelle ;
He prays that about midnight he may tell his matins.	He myȝt aboute myd-nyȝt,
2188	þe dele his matynnes telle !"

IX.

"Truly," says Sir Gawayne, "a desert is here,	" Now I-wysse," quoth Wowayn, "wysty is here ;
	þis oritore is vgly, with erbeȝ ouer-growen ;
a fitting place for the man in green	Wel bisemeȝ þe wyȝe wruxled in grene
to 'deal here his devotions in devil fashion.' 2192	Dele here his deuocioun, on þe deueleȝ wyse ;
	Now I fele hit is þe fende, in my fyue wytteȝ,
	þat hatȝ stoken me þis steuen, to strye me here ;
It is the most cursed kirk that ever I entered." 2196	þis is a chapel of meschaunce, þat chekke hit by-tyde,
	Hit is þe corsedest kyrk, þat euer I com inne !"
[Fol. 120b.]	With heȝe helme on his hede, his launce in his houde,
Roaming about he hears a loud noise,	He romeȝ vp to þe rokke of þo roȝ woneȝ ;
	þene herde he of þat hyȝe hil, in a harde roche,
from beyond the brook. 2200	Biȝonde þe broke, in a bonk, a wonder breme noyse,
It clattered like the grinding of a scythe on a grind-stone.	Quat ! hit clatered in þe clyff, as hit cleue schulde,
	As one vpon a gryndelston hade grounden a syþe ;
It whirred like a mill-stream.	What ! hit wharred, & whette, as water at a mulne,
2204	What ! hit rusched, & ronge, rawþe to here.
	þenne "bi godde," quoth Gawayn, "þat gere as² I trowe,
	Is ryched at þe reuerence, me renk to mete,
	bi rote ;
2208	Let god worche we loo,
"Though my life I forego," says the knight, "no noise shall terrify me."	Hit helppeȝ me not a mote,
	My lif þaȝ I for-goo,
	Drede dotȝ me no lote."

X.

Then cried he aloud, "Who dwells here, discourse with me to hold !"	2212 Thenne þe knyȝt con calle ful hyȝe,
	" Who stiȝtleȝ in þis sted, me steuen to holde ?

¹ wel (?).   ² at, in MS.

For now is gode Gawayn goande ryȝt here,

If any wyȝe oȝt wyl wynne hider fast,

2216 Oþer now, oþer neuer, his nedeȝ to spede."

"Abyde," quoth on on þe bonke, abouen ouer his hede,

" & þou schal haf al in hast, þat I þe hyȝt ones."

ȝet he rusched on þat rurde, rapely a þrowe,

2220 & wyth quettyng a-wharf, er he wolde lyȝt ;

& syþen he keuereȝ bi a cragge, & comeȝ of a hole,

Whyrlande out of a wro, wyth a felle weppen,

A deneȝ ax nwe dyȝt, þe dynt with [t]o ȝelde

2224 With a borelych bytte, bende by þe halme,

Fyled in a fylor, fowre fote large, .

Hit watȝ no lasse, bi þat lace þat lemed ful bryȝt.

& þe gome in þe grene gered as fyrst,

2228 Boþe þe lyre & þe leggeȝ, lokkeȝ, & berde,

Saue þat fayre on his fote he foundeȝ on þe erþe,

Sette þe stele to the stone, & stalked bysyde.

When he wan to þe watter, þer he wade nolde,

2232 He hypped ouer on hys ax, & orpedly strydeȝ,

Bremly broþe on a bent, þat brode watȝ a-boute,

on snawe.

Syr Gawayn þe knyȝt con mete,

2236   He ne lutte hym no þyng lowe,

þat oþer sayde, " now, syr swete,

Of steuen mon may þe trowe."

XI.

"Gawayn," quoth þat grene gome, "god þe mot loke !

2240 I-wysse þou art welcom,[1] wyȝe, to my place,

& þou hatȝ tymed þi trauayl as true[2] mon schulde ;

& þou knoweȝ þe couenaunteȝ kest vus by-twene,

At þis tyme twelmonyth þou toke þat þe falled,

2244 & I schulde at þis nwe ȝere ȝeply þe quyte.

& we ar in þis valay, verayly oure one,

Here ar no renkes vs to rydde, rele as vus likeȝ ;

---

[1] welcon, in MS.   [2] truee, in MS.

72   GAWAYNE PREPARES FOR THE BLOW.

Have off thy
helmet and take
thy pay at once."

Haf þy þy helme of þy hede, & haf here þy pay;
2248 Busk no more debate þen I þe bede þenne,
When þou wypped of my hede at a wap one."

"By God," quoth
Sir Gawayne, "I
shall not be-
grudge thee thy
will."

"Nay, bi god," quoth Gawayn, "þat me gost lante,
I schal gruch þe no grwe, for grem þat falleȝ;
2252 Bot styȝtel þe vpon on strok, & I schal stonde stylle,
& warp þe no wernyng, to worch as þe lykeȝ,
       no whare."

Then he shows
his bare neck,

      He lened with þe nek, & lutte,
2256 & schewed þat schyre al bare,
     & lette as he noȝt dutte,

and appears un-
daunted.

For drede he wolde not dare.

XII.

Then the man in
green seizes his
grim tool.

Then þe gome in þe grene grayþed hym swyþe,
2260 Gedereȝ vp hys grymme tole, Gawayn to smyte;

With all his force
he raises it aloft.

With alle þe bur in his body he ber hit on lofte,
Munt as maȝtyly, as marre hym he wolde;
Hade hit dryuen adoun, as dreȝ as he atled,
2264 Þer hade ben ded of his dynt, þat doȝty watȝ euer.
Bot Gawayn on þat giserne glyfte hym bysyde,

As it came gliding
down,

As hit com glydande adoun, on glode hym to schende,

Sir Gawayne
shrank a little
with his shoul-
ders.

& schranke a lytel with þe schulderes, for þe scharp yrne.
2268 Þat oþer schalk wyth a schunt þe schene wyth-haldeȝ,

The other re-
proved him, say-
ing,

& þenne repreued he þe prynce with mony prowde wordeȝ:

"Thou art not
Gawayne that is
so good esteemed,

"Þou art not Gawayn," quoth þe gome, "þat is so goud halden,
Þat neuer arȝed for no here, by hylle ne be vale,

[Fol. 121b.]

2272 & now þou fles for ferde, er þou fele harmeȝ;

for thou fleest for
fear before thou
feelest harm.
I never flinched
when thou
struckest.

Such cowardise of þat knyȝt cowþe I neuer here.
Nawþer fyked I, ne flaȝe, freke, quen þou myntest,
Ne kest no kauelacoun, in kyngeȝ hous Arthor,

My head flew to
my foot, yet I
never fled,

2276 My hede flaȝ to my fote, & ȝet flaȝ I neuer;
& þou, er any harme hent, arȝeȝ in hert,

Wherfore þe better burne me burde be called
   þer-fore."

wherefore I
ought to be called
the better man."

2280   Quoth G :, " I schunt oneȝ,
   & so wyl I no more,
   Bot þaȝ my hede falle on þe stoneȝ,
   I con not hit restore.

"I shunted once,"
says Gawayne,
" but will no
more.

XIII.

2284 Bot busk, burne, bi þi fayth, & bryng me to þe poynt,   Bring me to the
point; deal me
my destiny at
once."
   Dele to me my destiné, & do hit out of honde,
   For I schal stonde þe a strok, & start no more,
   Til þyn ax haue me hitte, haf here my trawþe."
2288 " Haf at þe þenne," quoth þat oþer, & heueȝ hit alofte,   " Have at thee,
then," says the
other.
   & wayteȝ as wroþely, as he wode were ;
   He mynteȝ at hym maȝtyly, bot not þe mon ryueȝ,   With that he aims
at him a blow.
   With-helde heterly h[i]s honde, er hit hurt myȝt.
2292 Gawayn grayþely hit bydeȝ, & glent with no membre,   Gawayne never
flinches, but
stands as still as
a stone.
   Bot stode stylle as þe ston, oþer a stubbe auþer,
   þat raþeled is in roche grounde, with roteȝ a hundreth.
   þen muryly efte con he mele, þe mon in þe grene,
2296 " So now þou hatȝ þi hert holle, hitte me bihou[e]s ;   "Now," says the
Green Knight, "I
must hit thee,
since thy heart is
whole."
   Halde þe now þe hyȝe hode, þat Arþur þe raȝt,
   & kepe þy kanel at þis kest, ȝif hit keuer may."
   G : ful gryndelly with greme þenne sayde,
2300 " Wy þresch on, þou þro mon, þou þreteȝ to longe,   "Thrash on,"
says the other.
   I hope þat þi hert arȝe wyth þyn awen seluen."
   "For soþe," quoth þat oþer freke, "so felly þou spekeȝ,
   I wyl no lenger on lyte lette þin ernde,
2304   riȝte nowe."
    þenne tas he[1] hym stryþe to stryke,   Then the Green
Knight makes
ready to strike.
    & frounses boþe lyppe & browe,
    No meruayle þaȝ hym myslyke,
2308   þat hoped of no rescowe.

      [1] he he, in MS.

XIV.

He let fall his

[Fol. 122.]

loom on the bare neck of Sir Gawayne.

The sharp weapon pierced the flesh so that the blood flowed.

When the knight saw the blood on the snow,

he unsheathed his sword, and thus spake:

"Cease, man, of thy blow.

If thou givest me any more, readily shall I requite thee.

Our agreement stipulates only one stroke."

He lyftes ly3tly his lome, & let hit dou*n* fayre,
With þe barbe of þe bitte bi þe bare nek ;
Þa3 he homered heter*ly*, hurt hy*m* no more,
2312 Bot snyrt hy*m* on þat on syde, þat seu*er*ed þe hyde ;
Þe scharp schrank to þe flesche þur3 þe schyre grece,
Þat þe schene blod o*uer* his schulderes schot to þe erþe.
& quen þe burne se3 þe blode blenk on þe snawe,
2316 He sprit forth spenne fote more þen a spere len*þe*,
Hent heter*ly* his helme, & on his hed cast,
Schot wit*h* his schuldere3 his fayre schelde vnd*er*,
Brayde3 out a bry3t sworde, & bremely he spoke3 ;
2320 Neu*er* syn þat he wat3 burne borne of his moder,
Wat3 he neu*er* i*n* þis worlde, wy3e half so blyþe :---
"Blyn*n*e, burne, of þy bur, bede me no mo ;
I haf a stroke i*n* þis sted wit*h*-oute stryf hent,
2324 & if þow reche3 me any mo, I redyly schal quyte,
& 3elde 3ederly a3ayn, & þ*er* to 3e tryst,
& foo ;
Bot on stroke here me falle3,
2328 Þe couenau*n*t schap ry3t soo,
[Sikered][1] i*n* Arþure3 halle3,
& þer-fore, hende, now hoo !"

XV.

The Green Knight rested on his axe,

looked on Sir Gawayne, who appeared bold and fearless,

and addressed him as follows :

"Bold knight, be not so wroth,

The haþel heldet hy*m* fro, & on his ax rested,
2332 Sette þe schaft vpon schore, & to þe scharp lened,
& loked to þe leude, þat on þe launde 3ede,
How þat do3ty dredles deruely þer stonde3,
Armed ful a3le3 ; i*n* hert hit hy*m* lyke3.
2336 Þenn he mele3 muryly, wyth a much steuen,
& wyth a r[a]ykande rurde he to þe renk sayde,
"Bolde burne, on þis bent be not so gryndel ;
No mon here vn-man*er*ly þe mys-boden habbe,
2340 Ne kyd, bot as couenau*n*de, at kynge3 kort schaped ;

[1] Illegible.

I hyȝt þe a strok, & þou hit hatȝ, halde þe wel payed,

I promised thee a stroke and thou hast it, be satisfied.

I relece þe of þe remnaunt, of ryȝtes alle oþer;

ȝif¹ I deliuer had bene, a boffet, paraunter,

2344 I couþe wroþeloker haf waret, [&] to þe haf wroȝt anger.²

I could have dealt worse with thee.

Fyrst I mansed þe muryly, with a mynt one,

& roue þe wyth no rof, sore with ryȝt I þe proferd,

For þe forwarde þat we fest in þe fyrst nyȝt,

[Fol. 122b.]
I menaced thee with one blow for the covenant between us on the first night.

2348 & þou trystyly þe trawþe & trwly me haldeȝ,

Al þe gayne þow me gef, as god mon schulde;

þat oþer munt for þe morne, mon, I þe profered,

þou kyssedes my clere wyf, þe cosseȝ me raȝteȝ,

Another I aimed at thee because thou kissedst my wife.

2352 For boþe two here I þe bede bot two bare myntes,

boute scaþe;

Trwe mon trwe restore,

þenne þar mon drede no waþe;

A true man should restore truly, and then he need fear no harm.

2356 At þe þrid þou fayled þore,

& þer-for þat tappe ta þe.

Thou failedst at the third time, and therefore take thee that tap. (See l. 1861.)

XVI.

For hit is my wede þat þou wereȝ, þat ilke wouen girdel,

Myn owen wyf hit þe weued, I wot wel forsoþe;

For my weed (woven by my wife) thou wearest.

2360 Now know I wel þy cosses, & þy costes als,

& þe wowyng of my wyf, I wroȝt it myseluen;

I know thy kisses and my wife's wooing.

I sende hir to asay þe, & sothly me þynkkeȝ,

On þe fautlest freke, þat euer on fote ȝede;

I sent her to try thee, and faultless I found thee.

2364 As perle bi þe quite pese is of prys more,

So is Gawayn, in god fayth, bi oþer gay knyȝteȝ.

Bot here yow lakked a lyttel, syr, & lewte yow wonted,

But yet thou sinnedst a little,

Bot þat watȝ for no wylyde werke, ne wowyng nauþer,

2368 Bot for ȝe lufud your lyf, þe lasse I yow blame."

for love of thy life."

þat oþer stif mon in study stod a gret whyle;

So agreued for greme he gryed with-inne,

Alle þe blode of his brest blende in his face,

Gawayne stands confounded.

2372 þat al he schrank for schome, þat þe schalk talked.

þe forme worde vpon folde, þat þe freke meled,—

¹ uf, in MS.　　² This word is doubtful.

"Cursed," he says, "be cowardice and covetousness both!"

Then he takes off the girdle and throws it to the knight.

He curses his cowardice,

and confesses himself to have been guilty of untruth.

[Fol. 123.]

"Corsed worth cowarddyse & couetyse boþe!
In yow is vylany & vyse, þat vertue disstryeȝ."
2376 Þenne he kaȝt to þe knot, & þe kest lawseȝ,
Brayde broþely þe belt to þe burne seluen:
"Lo! þer þe falssyng, foule mot hit falle!
For care of þy knokke cowardyse me taȝt
2380 To a-corde me with couetyse, my kynde to for-sake,
þat is larges & lewte, þat longeȝ to knyȝteȝ.
Now am I fawty, & falce, & ferde haf been euer;
Of trecherye & vn-trawþe boþe bityde sorȝe
2384   & care!
I bi-knowe yow, knyȝt, here stylle,
Al fawty is my fare,
Leteȝ me ouer-take your wylle,
2388   & efte I schal be ware."

XVII.

Then the other, laughing, thus spoke:

"Thou art confessed so clean,

that I hold thee as pure as if thou hadst never been guilty.

I give thee, sir, the gold-hemmed girdle,

as a token of thy adventure at the Green Chapel. Come again to my abode, and abide there for the remainder of the festival."

Thenn loȝe þat oþer leude, & luflyly sayde,
"I halde hit hardily[1] hole, þe harme þat I hade;
þou art confessed so clene, be-knowen of þy mysses,
2392 & hatȝ þe penaunce apert, of þe poynt of myn egge,
I halde þe polysed of þat plyȝt, & pured as clene,
As þou hadeȝ neuer forfeted, syþen þou watȝ fyrst borne.
& I gif þe, syr, þe gurdel þat is golde hemmed;
2396 For hit is grene as my goune, syr G:, ȝe maye
þenk vpon þis ilke þrepe, þer þou forth þryngeȝ
Among prynces of prys, & þis a pure token
Of þe chaunce of þe grene chapel, at cheualrous knyȝteȝ;
2400 & ȝe schal in þis nwe ȝer aȝayn to my woneȝ,
& we schyn reuel þe remnaunt of þis ryche fest,
          ful bene."
þer laþed hym fast þe lorde,
2404   & sayde, "with my wyf, I wene,
We schal yow wel acorde,
þat watȝ your enmy kene."

[1] hardilyly, in MS.

XVIII.

"Nay, for soþe," q*uoth* þe segge, & sesed hys helme,

2408 & hatȝ hit of hendely, & þe haþel þonkkeȝ,

"I haf soiorned sadly, sele yow bytyde,

& he ȝelde hit ȝow ȝare, þat ȝarkkeȝ al me*n*skes!

& comaundeȝ me to þat cortays, yo*ur* comlych fere,

2412 Boþe þat on & þat oþ*er*, myn honou*r*ed ladyeȝ,

þat þ*us* hor knyȝt wyth hor kest han koy*n*tly bigyled.

Bot hit is no ferly, þaȝ a fole madde,

& þurȝ wyles of wy*m*men be wonen to sorȝe ;

2416 For so watȝ Adam i*n* erde w*ith* one bygyled,

& Salamon w*ith* fele sere, & Samson eft soneȝ,

Dalyda dalt hy*m* hys wyrde, & Dauyth þ*er-aft*er

Watȝ blended w*ith* Barsabe, þat much bale þoled.

2420 Now þese were wrathed wyth her wyles, h*it* were a
　　　wy*n*n'e huge,

To luf hom wel, & leue hem not, a leude þat couþe,

For þes wer forne[1] þe freest þat folȝed alle þe sele,

Ex-ellently of alle þyse oþ*er*, vnder heue*n*-ryche,

2424　　　þat mused ;

　　& alle þay were bi-wyled,

　　With[2] wy*m*men þat þay vsed,

　　þaȝ I be now bigyled,

2428　Me þink me burde be excused."

XIX.

"Bot your gordel," q*uoth* G : "god yow for-ȝelde !

þat wyl I welde wyth good wylle, not for þe wy*n*ne
　　golde,

Ne þe saynt, ne þe sylk, ne þe syde pendau*n*des,

2432 For wele, ne for worchyp, ne for þe wlonk werkkeȝ,

Bot i*n* sygne of my surfet I schal se hit ofte ;

When I ride i*n* renou*n*, remorde to myselue*n*

þe faut & þe fayntyse of þe flesche crabbed,

[Side notes:]

---

[1] forme (?).　　　　　　[2] with wyth, in MS.

2436 How tender hit is to entyse teches of fylþe;

And when pride shall prick me,

& þus, quen pryde schal me pryk, for prowes of armes,

a look to this lace shall abate it.

þe loke to þis luf lace schal leþe my hert.

Bot on I wolde yow pray, displeses yow neuer;

2440 Syn ȝe be lorde of the ȝonder londe, þer I haf lent inne,

Wyth yow wyth worschyp,—þe wyȝe hit yow ȝelde

þat vp-haldeȝ þe heuen, & on hyȝ sitteȝ,—

But tell me your right name and I shall have done."

How norne ȝe yowre ryȝt nome, & þenne no more?"

2444 "þat schal I telle þe trwly," quoth þat oþer þenne,

The Green Knight replies, "I am called Bernlak de Hautdesert, through might of Morgain la Fay,

"Bernlak de Hautdesert I hat in þis londe,

þurȝ myȝt of Morgne la Faye, þat in my hous lenges,

&[1] koyntyse of clergye, bi craftes wel lerned,

the pupil of Merlin.

2448 þe maystres of Merlyn, mony ho[2] taken;

For ho hatȝ dalt drwry ful dere sum tyme,

With þat conable klerk, þat knowes alle your knyȝteȝ

at hame;

2452 Morgne þe goddes,

þerfore hit is hir name;

She can tame even the haughtiest.

Weldeȝ non so hyȝe hawtesse,

þat ho ne con make ful tame.

XX.

It was she who caused me to test the renown of the Round Table,

2456 Ho wayned me vpon þis wyse to your wynne halle,

For to assay þe surquidre, ȝif hit soth were,

þat rennes of þe grete renoun of þe Rounde Table;

Ho wayned me þis wonder, your wytteȝ to reue,

[Fol. 124.]

hoping to grieve Guenever and cause her death through fear.

2460 For to haf greued Gaynour, & gart hir to dyȝe,

With gopnyng[3] of þat ilke gomen, þat gostlych speked,

With his hede in his honde, bifore þe hyȝe table.

þat is ho þat is at home, þe auncian lady;

She is even thine aunt.

2464 Ho is euen þyn aunt, Arþureȝ half suster,

þe duches doȝter of Tyntagelle, þat dere Vter after

Therefore come to her and make merry in my house."

Hade Arþur vpon, þat aþel is nowþe.

þerfore I eþe þe, haþel, to com to þy naunt,

---

[1] in (?).   [2] ho hatȝ (?).   [3] glopnyng (?).

2468   Make myry in my hous, my meny þe louies,
      & I wol þe as wel, wyȝe, bi my faythe,
      As any gome vnder god, for þy grete trauþe."

      & he nikked hym naye, he nolde bi no wayes;

Gawayne refuses to return with the Green Knight.

2472 þay acolen & kyssen, [bikennen] ayþer oþer
      To þe prynoe of paradise, & parten ryȝt þere,
          on coolde;

      Gawayn on blonk ful bene,

On horse full fair he bends to Arthur's hall.

2476   To þe kynge; bur; buske; bolde,
      & þe knyȝt in þe enker grene,
      Whiderwarde so euer he wolde.

XXI.

      Wylde wayeȝ in þe worlde Wowen now rydeȝ,

Wild ways now Gawayne rides.

2480 On Gryngolet, þat þe grace hade geten of his lyue;
      Ofte he herbered in house, & ofte al þeroute,

Oft he harboured in house and oft thereout.

      & mony a-venture in vale, & venquyst ofte,
      þat I ne tyȝt, at þis tyme, in tale to remene.

2484 þe hurt watȝ hole, þat he hade hent in his nek,

The wound in his neck became whole.

      & þe blykkande belt he bere þeraboute,
      A belef as a bauderyk, bounden bi his syde,

He still carried about him the belt,

      Loken vnder his lyfte arme, þe lace, with a knot,

2488 In tokenyng he watȝ tane in tech of a faute;

in token of his fault.

      & þus he commes to þe court, knyȝt al in sounde.

Thus he comes to the Court of King Arthur.

      þer wakned wele in þat wone, when wyst þe grete,
      þat gode G : watȝ commen, gayn hit hym þoȝt;

Great then was the joy of all.

2492 þe kyng kysseȝ þe knyȝt, & þe whene alce,

The king and his knights ask him concerning his journey.

      & syþen mony syker knyȝt, þat soȝt hym to haylce,
      Of his fare þat hym frayned, & ferlyly he telles;

Gawayne tells them of his adventures,

      Bi-knoweȝ alle þe costes of care þat he hade,—

2496 þe chaunce of þe chapel, þe chere of þe knyȝt,
      þe luf of þe ladi, þe lace at þe last.

[Fol. 124b.] the love of the lady, and lastly of the lace.

      þe nirt in þe nek he naked hem schewed,

He showed them the cut in his neck.

      þat he laȝt for his vnleute at þe leudes hondes,

2500   for blame;

He tened quen he schulde telle,

He groned for gref & grame;

þe blod in his face con melle,

2504   When he hit schulde schewe, for schame.

XXII.

"Lo! lorde," quoth þe leude, & þe lace hondeled,

"þis is þe bende of þis blame I bere [in] my nek,

þis is þe laþe & þe losse, þat I laȝt haue,

2508   Of couardise & couetyse, þat I haf caȝt þare,

þis is þe token of vn-trawþe, þat I am tan inne,

& I mot nedeȝ hit were, wyle I may last;

For non may hyden his harme, bot vnhap ne may hit,

2512   For þer hit oneȝ is tachched, twynne wil hit neuer."

þe kyng comforteȝ þe knyȝt, & alle þe court als,

Laȝen loude þer-at, & luflyly acorden,

þat lordes & ladis, þat longed to þe Table,

2516   Vche burne of þe broþer-hede a bauderyk schulde haue,

A bende, a belef hym a-boute, of a bryȝt grene,

& þat, for sake of þat segge, in swete to were.

For þat watȝ acorded þe renoun of þe Rounde Table,

2520   & he honoured þat hit hade, euer-more after,

As hit is breued in þe best boke of romaunce.

þus in Arthurus day þis aunter bitidde,

þe Brutus bokees þer-of beres wyttenesse;

2524   Syþen Brutus, þe bolde burne, boȝed hider fyrst,

After þe segge & þe asaute watȝ sesed at Troye,

I-wysse;

Mony auntereȝ here bi-forne,

2528   Haf fallen suche er þis:

Now þat bere þe croun of þorne,

He bryng vus to his blysse! AMEN.

Side notes:

He groaned for grief and shame, and the blood rushed into his face.

"Lo!" says he, handling the lace, "this is the band of blame,

a token of my cowardice and covetousness.

I must needs wear it as long as I live."

The king comforts the knight, and all the court too.

Each knight of the brotherhood agrees to wear a bright green belt,

for Gawayne's sake,

who ever more honoured it.

Thus in Arthur's day this adventure befell.

He that bore the crown of thorns bring us to His bliss!

NOTES.

Page 2. l. 37. *þis kyng lay at Camylot vpon kryst-masse.*
Camalot, in Malory's "Morte Arthure," is said to be the same as Winchester. Ritson supposes it to be *Caer-went*, in Monmouthshire, and afterwards confounded with *Caer-wynt*, or *Winchester*. But popular tradition here seems the best guide, which assigned the site of Camalot to the ruins of a castle on a hill, near the church of South Cadbury, in Somersetshire (Sir F. Madden).

P. 3. l. 65 *Nowel nayted o-newe, neuened ful ofte.*
Christmas celebrated anew, mentioned full often.
Sir F. Madden leaves the word *nayted* unexplained in his Glossary to "Syr Gawayne."

P. 5. l. 124 *syluener = sylueren*, *i.e.* silver dishes. 139 *lyndes = lendes*, loins. 142 *in his muckel*, in his greatness.

P. 7. l. 216 *in gracons werkes.* Sir F. Madden suggests *Greek* as the meaning of *gracons.* I am inclined to look upon *gracons* as an error for *gracous = gracious*, *i.e.* fair, beautiful, a very common meaning of the term.

P. 8. ll. 244–5 *As al were slypped vpon slepe so slaked hor lotez in hyȝe.*
As all were fallen asleep so ceased their words in haste (suddenly).
Sir F. Madden reads *slaked horlotez*, instead of *slaked hor lotez*, which, according to his glossary, signifies drunken vagabonds. He evidently takes *horlotez* to be another (and a very uncommon) form of *harlotez = harlots.* But *harlot*, or vagabond, would be a very inappropriate term to apply to the *Knights of the Round Table.* Moreover, *slaked* never, I think, means drunken. The general sense of the verb *slake* is to let loose, lessen, cease. Cf. lines 411–2, where *sloke*, another form of *slake*, occurs with a similar meaning : —————— *layt no fyrre ;*
bot slokes.
—————— seek no further,
but stop (cease).
Sir F. Madden suggests *blows* as the explanation of *slokes.* It is, however, a *verb* in the imperative mood.

6

P. 13. l. 394 *siker*. Sir F. Madden reads *swer*.

P. 14. l. 440 *bluk*. Sir F. Madden suggests *blunk* (horse). I am inclined to keep to the reading of the MS., and explain *bluk* as = *bulk* = trunk. Cf. the use of the word *Blok* in "Early English Alliterative Poems," p. 100, l. 272.

P. 18. l. 558 *derue doel*, etc. = great grief. Sir F. Madden reads *derne, i.e.* secret, instead of *derue* (= *derf*). Cf. line 564.

P. 20. l. 629   *& ay quere hit is eindeleȝ*, etc.
           And everywhere it is *endless*, etc.
Sir F. Madden reads *emdeleȝ, i.e.* with equal sides.

P. 21. l. 652 *for-be* = *for-bi* = surpassing, beyond.

P. 22. l. 681 for *Hadet* read *Halet* = *haled* = exiled (?). See line 1049.

P. 26. l. 806 *auinant* = *auenaunt*, pleasantly. Sir F. Madden reads *avnant*.

P. 30. l. 954 *of* Should we not read *on* (?).

P. 31. l. 957   *þat oþer wyth a gorger watȝ gered ouer þe swyre.*
The *gorger* or *wimple* is stated first to have appeared in Edward the First's reign, and an example is found on the monument of Aveline, Countess of Lancaster, who died in 1269. From the poem, however, it would seem that the *gorger* was confined to elderly ladies (Sir F. Madden).

968   *More lykker-wys on to lyk,*
          Watȝ þat scho had on lode.
       A more pleasant one to like,
       Was that (one) she had under her control.

P. 32. l. 888 *tayt* = lively, and hence pleasant, agreeable. 1015 *in vayres*, in purity.

P. 33. l. 1020 *dut* = *dunt* (?) = *dint* (?), referring to *sword-sports*. 1022 *sayn[t] Ioneȝ day*. This is the 27th of December, and the last of the feast. Sometimes the Christmas festivities were prolonged to New Year's Day (Sir F. Madden). 1047 *derne dede* = secret deed. I would prefer to read *derue dede* = great deed. Cf. lines 558, 564.

P. 34. l. 1053 *I wot in worlde*, etc. = *I [ne] wot in worlde*, etc.

1054   *I nolde, bot if I hit negh myȝt on nwȝeres morne,*
         For alle þe londe in-wyth Logres, etc.
I would not [delay to set out], unless I might approach it on New Year's morn, for all the lands within England, etc. 1074 *in spenne* = *in space* = in the interval = meanwhile. See line 1503.

P. 37. l. 1160 *slentyng of arwes*. Sir F. Madden reads *sleutyng*.
       "Of drawyn swerdis *sclentyng* to and fra,
        The brycht mettale, and othir armouris seir,
        Quharon the sonnys blenkis betis cleir,
        Glitteris and schane, and vnder bemys brycht
        Castis ane new twynklyng or a lemand lycht."
                      (G. Douglas' Æneid, Vol. i., p. 421.)

P. 41. l. 1281 *let lyk* = appeared pleased.

1283 *Þaȝ I were burde bryȝtest, þe burde in mynde hade,* etc.
The sense requires us to read :
Þaȝ ho were burde bryȝtest, þe burne in mynde hade, etc.
i.e., Though she were lady fairest, the knight in mind had, etc.

P. 46. l. 1440 *Long sythen [scuered] for þe sounder þat wiȝt for-olde*
Long since separated from the *sounder* or herd that fierce (one) for-aged
(grew very old).

" Now to speke of the boore, the fyrste year he is
A pygge of the *sounder* callyd, as haue I blys ;
The secounde yere an hogge, and soo shall he be,
And an hoggestere, whan he is of yeres thre ;
And when he is foure yere, a boor shall he be,
From the *sounder* of the swyne thenne departyth he ;
A synguler is he soo, for alone he woll go."
(Book of St. Alban's, ed. 1496, sig. *d.*, i.)

P. 52. l. 1623 A verb seems wanting after *lowde.*

P. 55. l. 1710 *a strothe rande* = a rugged path. Cf. the phrases *tene greue,* l. 1707 ;
roȝe greue, l. 1898. 1729 *bi lag* = *be-lagh* (?) = below (?).

1719 *Thenne watȝ hit lif vpon list,* etc.
Should we not read :
Thenne watȝ hit list vpon lif, etc.
i.e., Then was there joy in life, etc.

P. 57. l. 1780 *lyf* = *lef* (?), beloved (one).

P. 60. l. 1869 *Ho hatȝ kyst þe knyȝt so toȝt.*
She has kissed the knight so courteous.
Sir F. Madden explains *toȝt,* promptly. *Toȝt* seems to be the same as the
Northumbrian *taght* in the following extract from the " Morte Arthure " :
" There come in at the fyrste course, before the kyng seluene,
Bare hevedys that ware bryghte, burnyste with sylver,
Alle with *taghte* mene and *towne* in togers fulle ryche."—(p. 15.)
The word *towne* (well-behaved) still exists in *wan-ton,* the original meaning
of which was ill-mannered, ill-bred.

P. 61. l. 1909 *bray houndeȝ* = *braþ houndeȝ, i.e.* fierce hounds.

P. 64. l. 1995 *He hatȝ nere þat he soȝt* = *He watȝ nere þat he soȝt* = He was near to
that which he sought.

P. 69. l. 2160 *gedereȝ þe rake* = takes the path or way.

2167 *þe skweȝ of þe scowtes skayued hym þoȝt.*
The shadows of the hills appeared wild (desolate) to him.
Sir F. Madden reads *skayned,* of which he gives no explanation. *Skayued*
= *skayfed,* seems to be the N. Prov. English *scafe,* wild. Scotch *schaivie,*
wild, mad. O.N. *skeifr.* Sw. *skef,* awry, distorted.

P. 70.   l. 2204 *ronge* = clattered.

         2211   *Drede doþ me no lote* =

                    No noise shall cause me to dread (fear).

P. 75.   l. 2357   *& þer-for þat tappe ta þe.*

                    And therefore take thee that tap.

        ta þe = take thee. Sir F. Madden reads *taþe* = *taketh.* See page 14, l. 413, where *ta þe* rhymes with *sothe.* We have no imperatives in *th* in this poem.

P. 76.   l. 2401 *We schyn reuel,* etc. Sir F. Madden reads *waech yn rewel.* But *schyn* = shall. See Glossary to "Alliterative Poems."

P. 79.   l. 2474 *on-coolde* = *on-colde* = *coldly* = sorrowfully. 2489 *in-counde* = *soundly,* well. Cf. *in-blande* = together; *in-lyche,* alike; *in-mydde,* amidst.

GLOSSARIAL INDEX.

[*For all words marked thus* (*) *the reader is referred to the Glossary to Early English Alliterative Poems.*]

Abataylment, battlement, 790.
Abloy, an exclamation used in hunting; equivalent to On! on! 1174. O.Fr. *ablo.*
Abof, above, 73, 112, 153.
Abouen, above, 2217.
Achaufed, warmed, 883.
Acheue, to obtain, arrive, 1107, 1838.
Acheued, *pret.* 1081, 1857.
Acoles, embraces, 1936.
Acolen, *pl. pres.* embrace, 2472.
Acorde, 2406.
Adoun, down, 254.
Afyaunce, trust, confidence, 642.
After, afterwards, 218.
*Aghlich, fearful, dreadful, 136.
Aker, field, plain, 1421. Sir F. Madden proposes to read *vch a* =every (each a).
Alce=alse, also, likewise, 2492.
Alder, elder, 973.
Alder-truest, truest of all, 1486.
Alderes=elders, ancestors, 95.
Algate, every way, 141.
Al-hal-day, All-hallows day, 1st November, 536.
Al one, alone, 735, 2155. *Al hym one=Al his one*, by himself, 749, 1048.
A-losed, praised, 1512. See *Los, Lose.*

Als, } also, likewise, 270, 720,
Alse, } 933, 1627.
Al-same, together, 673.
Alther-grattest, greatest of all, 1441.
Aluisch = elvish, having preternatural power. A.S. *ælf, elf,* an elf, sprite, genius.
Amende, 898.
Amongeȝ, amongst, 1361.
Amount, 1197.
Anamayld, enamelled, 169.
And=an, if, 1245, 1509, 1647.
Ane, one, 223.
A-nelede, attacked, worried, 723. Sir F. Madden renders it *approached.*
Angardeȝ, arrogance, 681.
Anious, wearisome, sorrowful, fatiguing, 535. O.Fr. *anieux, anieuse.* Lat. *anxius.*
Another, otherwise, 1268.
Apendes, } appertains, belongs,
Apendeȝ, } 623, 913.
Apert, openly, manifestly, 154, 2392.
Apparayl, 600, 1891.
Aray, 163.
Are, ere, before, previously, 239. 1632.
A-rered, retreated, 1902.

Arewe₃, } arrows, 1160, 1455,
Arwes, } 1460.
Arwe₃, }
Armure, 586.
Arꞇ, are (pl. pres.), 280, 1094.
Arsoune₃, } saddle-bows, 171, 602.
Arsoun₃, }
*Ar₃e, timid, fearful, 241.
Ar₃e, vb. to wax timid, 2301.
Ar₃ed, waxed timid, 1463, 2271.
Ar₃e₃, waxest timid, 2277.
Asay, the point in the breast of
the buck, at which the hunter's
knife was inserted, to make trial
of the animal's fatness, 1328.
Asay, try, tempt, 2362.
*Ascryed, shouted, 1153.
*Aske₃, ashes, 2.
Askyng, request, 323, 349.
Asoyled, absolved, 1883.
Aspye, to discover, 1199.
Assaut, assault, 1.
As-swythe, quickly, 1400.
*As-tit, } at once, suddenly, 31,
As-tyt, } 1210. See Tit, Tite.
At, for, 648; of, 703.
*Athel, noble, good, 5, 171, 241,
904, 1654, 2466.
Ather=ayther, either, 1357.
*Attle, vb. aim, design, purpose, 27.
Attled, pret. of attle, 2263.
*At-waped, escaped, 1167. See
Wapped.
Auen, }
Awen, } own, 10, 293, 836.
Aune, }
*Auinant = avinaunt, avenaunt,
pleasantly, 806.
Aumayl, enamel, 236.
Auncian, adj. aged, 1001, 2463;
sb. aged (one), 948.
*Aunter, adventure, 27, 29, 2522.
Auntere₃ (pl.), 2527.
Auntered, ventured, 1516.
Auther, either, 88, 702.
A-vanters, portions of the nombles
of a deer, which lay near the

neck; a term used in woodcraft, 1342.
"Then dresse the nombles, fyrst that
ye recke;
Downe the auancers kerue, that cleuyth
to the neck;
And down wyth the bol-throte put
theym anone."
(Boke of St. Alban's, 1496, sig. d. iv.)
"One croke of the nombles lyeth
euermore
Under the throte-bolle of the beest
before,
That callyd is auauncers, whoso can
theym kenne."
(Ibid., sig. e. i.)
Auentale, the open and moveable
portion of the helmet which
covered the mouth, for the pur-
pose of respiration, 608.
"He brayedez one a bacenett, bur-
neschte of syluer,
The beste that was in Basille, wyth
bordurs ryche;
The creste and the coronalle enclosed
so faire,
Wyth clasppis of clere golde, couched
wyth stones;
The vesare, the aventaile, enarmede so
faire,
Voyde with owttyne vice, with wyn-
dowes of syluer."
(Morte Arthure, p. 77.)
"The vesere, the auentaile, his ves-
turis ryche,
Wyth the valyant blode was verrede
alle over."
(Ibid., p. 215.)
Early writers frequently use this
term for the whole front of the
helmet, including the visor. In
the prose French romances of the
Round Table, ventaille is a dis-
tinct piece of armour, and put
on before the helmet.
Auenturus, adventurous, 93.
Auenturus, adventures, 95, 491.
Auinant, pleasantly, 806.
A-vyse, } think, devise, 45, 1389.
Awyse, }
Auysed, viewed, observed, 771.

A-wharf, turned, whirled round, 2220. A.S. *a-hweorfan*, to bend (*pret. a-hwearf.*)

Ax, 208.

Ay, ever, 26, 73, 128, 167, 893.

Ayled, 438.

Ay-quere,) everywhere, 599,629,
Ay-where,) 745, 800.

Ayther, either, 841, 939, 1307.

Aȝayn,) towards, 815, 971;
Aȝaynes,)
Aȝayneȝ,) against, 1456, 1661.

*Aȝleȝ, fearless, 2335. See *Aghlich.*

Aȝt, aȝte, owned, possessed (the *pret.* of *awe,* to own, owe), 767, 843, 1775, 1941.

Bade, abode, tarried, 1699.

Baldly, boldly, 376.

*Bale, harm, evil, grief, 2041, 2419.

Bale, belly, 1333. O.H.G. *balg.*

Baleȝ, bowels, 1333.

Balȝe, round or smooth, 2032, 2172. "*Balhew* or pleyn (*balwe* or playne, P.) Planus." (Prompt. Parv.)

Bande, 192.

Baner, 117.

Barayne, barren, applied to hinds not gravid, 1320.

Barhe, edge of an axe, 2310.

Barbeȝ, points of arrows, 1457.

Barbican, out-work or tower of a castle, 793.

*Bare, *adj.* mere, unconditional, 277. In l. 1141 it is applied to the motes or blasts of a horn, and seems to mean *short* or *without rechate*; *adv.* 465; "*bare* þre dayeȝ," 1066.

Barely, unconditionally, certainly, 548.

Baret, strife, contest, 21, 353, 2115; grief, 752.

Bargayn, 1112.

Barlay, Sir F. M. says, is apparently a corruption of the

French *par loi,* 296. Is it a corruption of the phrase, "by our lady," *i.e.* the Virgin Mary?

Barred, striped diagonally, 159.

Barres, diagonal stripes, 162.

Bastel-roueȝ, turreted or castellated roofs; *roueȝ* = roofs.

Bate, debate, conflict, 1461. A.S. *bate,* contention.

Bauderyk, the strap by which the shield was suspended round the neck, 621; belt or lace, 2486. M.H.G. *balderich.*

Bawe, bow of a saddle (?), 435.

Bawe-men, bowmen, 1564.

Bay, round, 967. A.S. *bugan,* to bend.

Bay,) bay or baiting of a wild
Baye,) boar, when attacked by dogs, 1450, 1564, 1582.

Bayed, baited, barked at, 1142, 1362, 1603.

Bayen (*3d pers. pl.*), bay, bark at, 1909.

*Bayn,) prompt, ready, obedient,
Bayne,) 1092, 2158.

Bayst, abashed, 37. Fr. *abaisser*

Baythe, to grant (?), 327; to consent, 1404, 1840.

Be, by, 652, 1216.

Beau, fair, 1222.

Be-com, went, 460.

Bedde,) offered, 1824, 1834, 2248.
Bede,)

Beddeȝ, bids, 1374.

Beddyng, 853.

Bede, bade, 1437, 2090.

Bede, offer, proffer, 374, 382, 2322 A.S. *beodan,* to offer.

Be-knewe, acknowledge.

Beknowen, acknowledged, 2391.

Belde, courage, valour, 650. A.S. *byld.*

Bele-chere, good company (*cheer*) or presence.

Belef, badge (?), 2486, 2517.

Belleȝ, bells, 195.

Belt, 162.

Bende, band, bond, 2505, 2517.

Bende, bent, 305, 2224; put down, 2105.

Bene, to be, 141; are or will be, 1646.

*Bene (another form of *bain*?), fair, well, 2402, 2475.

*Bent, plain, field (or uplands?), 353, 1465, 1599, 2115, 2233, 2338; "*bent-field*," 1136.

Ber, beer, 129.

Ber, } bore, carried, 637, 1913.
Bere, }

Berdleʒ, 280.

Berʒ, } hill, mount, 2172, 2178.
Berʒe, }

Best, beast, animal, 1436.

*Bete, to kindle, 1367.

Beten, worked, embroidered, 78, 1833, 2028. Fr. *battu*.

Beuerage, drink, liquor, 1112, 1409.

Beuer-hwed = beaver-hued, colour of a beaver (?), 845.

Bide, } abide, endure, 374, 520,
Byde, } 1582, 2041.

Bideʒ, } abides, awaits, 376.
Bydeʒ, }

Bifalleʒ, 382.

Biforne, before, 123.

Big, bold, 354.

*Biges, builds, 9.

*Bigged, } built, inhabited, 20.
Bygged, }

*Bigly, } loudly, 1141; deeply,
*Bygly, } severely, 1162; boldly, 1584.

Bigrauen, engraved, 216.

Bi-grypte = be-gripped, grasped, 214.

Bihalden, } = beholden, indebted,
Biholde, } 1557, 1842.

Bi-hond, forthwith, 67.

Bihoues, 1065.

Bikende, commended, 596, 1982.

Biknowe, acknowledge, 2385.

Biknoweʒ, acknowledges, 2495.

*Biliue, } quickly, immediately,
Bilyue, } 132, 1128, 1136, 1171,
Bylyue, } 1715.

Bisemed, befitted, became, 622, 2035.

Bisemeʒ = beseems, befits. 1612, 2191.

Bisides, } = besides, on the side,
Bisydeʒ, } 76, 109, 856.

Bisied, agitated, 89.

Bisoʒt, besought, 96.

Bitidde, befell, 2522.

Bitte, } the steel part of an axe,
Bytte, } 2224, 2310.

*Bi-wyled, beguiled, 2425.

*Blande, intermixed, blended; phrase "*in blande*," together, 1205, 1931.

Blasoun, shield of arms, 828.

Blaunner, } a species of fur (?),
Blaunier, } 155, 573, 856, 1931. Is it connected with *lawn*?—if so, it would signify a species of fine linen.

*Bleaunt, } a robe or mantle (of fine
Bleeant, } linen), 879, 1928.

Blenched, receded, drew back, 1715.

Blende = blent, mingled, blended, 1361, 1610, 2371.

Blenk, to shine, 2315. Du. *blincken*, to shine, glitter. Ger. *blinken*, twinkle, glitter.

Blenked, shone, 799.

Blered, 963.

Blessing, 370.

*Blonk, } a steed, literally, a
Blonkke, } *white* horse, 434, 785, 1581.

Blonkes, } horses, 1128, 1693
Blonkkes, }

*Blubred = foamed, blubbered, applied to a stream of water, 2174

Bluk = trunk, 440.

Blunder, confusion, trouble, 18.

*Blunk, steed, 440. See *Blonk*.

*Blusch, *sb.* look, 520.

Bluschcd, looked, 650, 793.

Blusschande=blushing, glittering, 1819.

Blw,
Blwe, } blew, 1141, 1362.

Blwe, blue, 1928.

*Blycande, } shining, glittering,
Blykkande, } 305, 2485.

Blykked, shone, glistened, 429.

Blynne, cease, 2322.

Blysse, fortune, prosperity, 18.

Blyþe, gay, bright, 155.

*Bobbaunce, boast, 9.

Bobbe, branch, 206.

Bode, bidding, proffer, 852, 1824. A.S. *bod*.

*Bode, abode, 785, 1564.

*Boden, *pass. part.* prayed, asked, 327. A.S. *beodan* (*p.p. boden*), to bid, offer.

Bolde, *sb.* bold (one), 21.

*Bole, trunk of a tree, 766.

*Bolne, to swell, 512.

Bonchef, gaiety (or perhaps innocence, purity), 1764.

*Bone, prayer, request, 327.

Bone-hostel, lodging, 776.

*Bonk, bank, height, 511, 700, 710, 785, 1571.

*Bonkkes, } heights, 14, 1562,
Bonkkeʒ, } 2077.

Bord,
Borde, } table, 481.

Borde, border, 610; *bordes* (*pl.*) 159.

*Bordeʒ = bourdeʒ (?), jests (?), 1954.

*Borelych = burly, huge, strong, 766, 2148, 2224.

*Borne=bourn, stream, 731, 1570, 2174.

Bornyst,
Burnyst, } burnished, 212, 582.

*Borʒ,
Borʒe, } =burgh, city, castle, 2,
Burʒ, } 9, 259, 843, 1092.
Burʒe, }

Bot-if, unless, 1782.

Bot, } bit, wounded, pierced, 426,
Bote, } 1162, 1562.

Bothem, bottom, 2145.

Botounʒ, buttons, 220.

*Boun, } ready, prompt, obedient,
Boune, } 548, 852, 1311, 1693.

Bour, chamber, 853, 1519.

*Bourde, sport, joke, 1409.

Bourdeʒ, jokes, 1212.

Bourded, joked, 1217.

Bourdyng, *sb.* joke, sport, 1404.

Bout, } without, 361, 1285, 1444.
Boute, }

*Boʒe, to move, rise, go, 344, 1220.

Boʒed (*pret.* of *boʒe*), 481, 550, 1189, 2524.

Boʒen (*pres. pl.* of *boʒe*), 434, 1311, 2077.

*Boʒes, goes, 2178.

Boʒeʒ, boughs, 765, 2077.

Brace, armour for the arms, 582.

Braches, } hounds, 1142, 1563,
Bracheʒ, } 1610. *Brache* is said to signify originally a bitch hound—the feminine of *rache*, a foot-scenting hound (Jam.).

Brachetes, hounds, 1603.

Brad, roasted, 891. A.S. *brædan*, to roast (*pret. brædde; p.p. gebræd*).

*Bradde, extended, 1928. See *Braide*.

*Braides, } draws, 621, 1584, 1609,
Braydes, } 1901.
Braydeʒ, }

Brawden, woven, 177, 580.

Brawen, } =brawn, or flesh of a
Brawne, } wild boar, 1611, 1631.

Bray, an error for *brath*, bold (?), 1909.

*Brayde, started, 429; threw, 2377; drew, 1399; drawn, thrown, 2069.

Brayden, embroidered, 220, 1883.

Brayn-wod, mad, violent, 286, 1461, 1580.

Bredden (*pl. pret.*)=bred, flourished. 21.

*Brede3, bounds, limits, 2071. A.S. *brerd*.

*Brem,) fierce, bold, 1142, 1155,
Breme,) 1580, 2200, loud, shrill,
1601; rugged, 2145.

*Breme,) quickly, boldly, 779,
Bremly,) 781; fiercely, 509,
Bremely,) 1598, 2233, 2319.
Bremlych,)

Brende,) burnt, burnished, 2,
Brenned,) 195, 832, 875, 2165.

Brenne3, burns, 1609.

*Brent, high, 2165.

*Bresed, rough, 305.

Brether, brethren, 39.

*Breue, tell, inform, speak, 1393, 1488.

Breued, marked, 1436; written, 2521.

Britned, broken or cut in pieces, 2, 680, 1339.

Britne3, breaks, cuts, 1611. A.S. *bryt-an*, to break.

Bronde,) sword, 561, 588, 828,
Bront) 1584.

Bronde3 = brands, embers, 2.

*Brothe, angry, fierce, 2233.

*Brothely, angrily, violently, 2377.

Brother-hede, brotherhood, 2516.

Broun, *sb.* brown (deer), 1162.

Browe, brow, 1457.

Bro3es,) brows, 305, 961.
Bro3e3,)

Bruny, cuirass, 861, 2012, 2018. A.S. *byrne*.

Brusten, burst, 1166.

Bryddes,) birds, 166, 509, 746.
Brydde3,)

Brygge, bridge, 779, 781.

*Brymme, flood, river, 2172.

Bugle, 1136.

Bult, built, 25.

*Bur, blow, 290, 374, 548, 2322; force, 2261.

*Burde, lady, 613, 752, 961.

Burdes,) ladies, 942, 1232, 1373.
Burde3,)

*Burde, ought, behoved, 2276, 2423.

*Burn,) man, knight, noble, 20,
Burne,) 73, 337.

Burne3,) men, 259, 272, 481.
Burne3,)

Burnyst, 212.

*Busk, array, 1220; prepare, 2243, 2284.

Busked, went, 1411; prepared, 1693.

Busken (*pl. pres.*), prepare, 509, 1128.

Buskes,) goes, 1136, 1448, 2476.
Buske3,)

Busk, bush, 182.

Buske3, bushes, 1437.

Busy, to be active, 1066.

Busyly, 68.

Buttoke3, 967.

Bycome, became, 6.

Bycomes, becomes, befits, 471.

Byforne, before, 1375, 1577.

Byhode, behoved, 717.

Bykende, commended, 569, 1982.

Bykennen, commend, 1307.

Bylde, 509.

Byled, boiled, 2082.

Bytoknyng, token, 626.

Caoh, to catch, take, acquire, 133; to go, 1794.

Cacheres = catchers, hunters, 1139.

Cache3 (*pres. tense* of *cach*), 368, 2175.

Can (*auxiliary vb.* of *past tense*), 340, 1042.

Capados, hood or close cap, from the Fr. *cap-à-dos*, 186, 572.

*Caple, horse, 2175.

Carande, sorrowing, anxious, 674, 750.

Care, grief, concern, 1979, 2379.

Carnele3, battlements, embrasures, 801.

Caroles, 43.

Carp, speech, conversation.

Carp,) to say, tell, speak, 263,
Karp,) 696, 704.
Carped, told, spoke, 1088.
Carppe꜓, tells, speaks, 377, 1979.
*Carye꜓ = cayre꜓, goes, 2120.
Cast, to speak, address, 249.
Castes, deeds, manners, 1295. See
Costes.
Cauelounꜛ=cauelaciounꜛ, disputes,
683, 2275. O.Fr. cavellation.
Cemmed = cammed (?), folded,
twisted, 188. O.E. cam, bent,
crooked.
Cercle, circle around the helmet,
615.
Chaffer, merchandise, 1647, 1939.
Chambre, 48.
Chaplayne, 930.
Charcole, 875.
Charg, matter, 1940.
Charge, vb. 863.
Chargeaunt, dangerous (?), 1604.
*Charre, return, 1678.
Charred, led, turned, 850, 1143.
Charres, business; task, 1674.
Chastysed, 1143.
Chauncely, accidentally, 778.
Chaunsel, 946.
Chauntre, religious service, 63.
O.F. chanterie.
Chefly,) speedily (?), 850, 883,
Cheuely,) 978, 1940.
Chek, fortune, 1107, 1857.
Chekke, ill fortune (?), 2195.
Chemne(=chimney),fireplace,978.
Chepe,) bargain, terms of buying
Chepe꜓,) or selling, or goods
sold, 1939, 1940, 1941.
Chepen, to bargain, 1271.
*Cher,) countenance, behaviour,
Chere,) spirits, 562, 711, 883,
1745, 2169, 2496; entertain-
ment, 1259.
Ches (=chose), perceived, dis-
cerned, 798, 946.
*Cheue, obtain, 1271; to arrive,
1676.

Cheued, obtained, 1390; came, 63.
Cheuicaunce,) booty, gain, 1390,
Cheuisaunce,) 1406,1678,1939.
Cheuysaunce,) O.Fr. cheuissance.
Cheyer, chair, 875.
Child-gered, of childish manners,
86 (literally=dressed as a child).
*Chorle, churl, 2107.
Chosen (the gate), took the way,
930.
"Towarde꜓ Chartris they chese these
cheualrous knyghttez."
(Morte Arthure, p. 136.)
Chylder, children, 280.
Chymbled, folded (?), 958. Is it
connected with Eng. chymb, from
Du. kimme, rim or edge of a
vase?
Clad, covered, 885.
Clamberande, clustering, 1722.
Clambered, clustered, joined to-
gether, 801.
Clanly, wholly, 393.
Clanness, chastity, purity, 653.
Clatterande (=clattering), bub-
bling, 731.
Clattered, resounded, 1722.
Clayme, 293.
Clene, fair, 163; wholly, 1298.
Clenge꜓ (=clings), contracts, or
causes to shrink with cold, 505,
2078.
Clenged, 1694, pret. of Clenge.
Clepes, calls, 1310.
Cler,) fine, fair, bright, beautiful,
Clere,) noble, 631, 942, 954,
1489.
Clergye, erudition, 2447.
Clomben, climbed, 2078.
Close, 186.
Closet, 934.
Cloyster, 804..
*Cofly, quickly, 2011.
Colén, to cool, assuage, 1253.
Com,) came (pl. comen), 116,
Come,) 824, 942, 1004.
Comaunde꜓, (imp.) commend, 2411.

Comly, } *adj.* comely, fair, 469,
Comlych, } 539; used substan-
tively, 674, 1755; used ad-
verbially, 648, 1307, 1629, 1794.
Comlyly, courteously, 974, 1118,
1389.
Comloker, comelier, 869.
Comlokest, most comely, 52, 81,
767.
Compass, form, stature, 944.
Compast, 1196.
Company, 556, 1011.
Con, } can, 2455.
Conne, }
Con, } an auxiliary vb. (of the
Conne, } past tense), 230, 274,
362, 841, 993, 1206.
Conne₃, knows, 1267, 1483.
Conable (=convenable), famous, or
accomplished, 2450. O.Fr. *co-
vinable.*
Concience, 1196.
Conquestes, 311.
Conueyed, 596.
Conysaunce, badge, cognisance,
2026.
*Coprounes, capitals, 797.
Corbeles, raven's, 1355.
Corner, 1185.
Cors, body, 1297.
Cors, course, 116.
Corsedest, most cursed, 2196.
Corsour, 1583.
Cortays, } courteous, 276, 467,
Cortayse, } 539.
Cortaysy, } courtesy, 247, 263,
Cortaysye, } 1300.
Cortaysly, courteously, 775, 903.
Cortyn, curtain, 854, 1185.
Cortyned, 1181.
Coruon, carved, 797.
Cosse, kiss, 1300.
Cosses, } kisses, 2351, 2360.
Cosse₃, }
Cost, manner, business, 546.
Costes, } manners, qualities, vir-
Coste₃, } tues, 944, 1272, 1483,

1489, 2360, 2495; labours, 750.
Icel. *kostr*, habits, character, con-
ditions. Ger. *kust*, art.
Coste₃, coasts, 1696.
Cosyn, 372.
Cote, 152, 335.
Cothe, quoth, 776.
Coundue, to conduct, guide, 1972.
O.Fr. *conduire.*
Coundutes, songs, 1655. O.Fr. *con-
duis.*
Counseyl, 557.
Countenaunce, custom, 100, 1490.
Couples, 1147.
Cource, 135.
Couth, } (=could), knew, 45,
Couthe, } 1125, 1139, 1389,
Cowthe, } 1486; known, 1490.
Couthly, familiarly, 937.
Couenaunt, 393.
Couertor, } cover or trapping of a
Couertour, } horse, 602; canopy
of a bed, 1181.
Couertore₃, canopies, 855.
Cowpled, 1139.
Cowters, pieces of plate for the
elbows, 583. Fr. *coudière*, la
partie qui covre la *coude.*
Coynt, } curious, quaint, 877;
Koynt, } skilful, cunning, 1525.
Coyntly, }
Coyntlych, } cunningly, 578, 934,
Koyntly, } 2413.
Co₃ed = coughed, 307.
Crabbed, 502.
Crafty, skilfully made, 572.
Crakkande, resounding, loud, 1166.
Crakkyng, blast, blowing, 116.
Cresped, crisped, 188.
Crathayn, craven, coward, 1773.
"Becum thow cowart *crawdoun* re-
cryand."
(G. Douglas, Vol. ii., p. 673.)
Crest, top of a rock, 731.
Creuisse, fissure, cavity, 2183.
Criande, crying, 1088.
Croked, bent aside, 653.

Cropore,) crupper, 168, 602.
Cropure,)
Croys, cross, 643.
Crystenmas, Christmas, 985.
Cummen, come, 60, 62.

Dabate=debate, strife, 2041.
Daly, to dally, 1253.
Dalt, dealt, fared, passed away time, 452, 1664, 2449.
Dalten (*pret. pl.*), 1114.
Dalyaunce, 1012.
Dar, dare, 287.
*Dare, to manifest fear, tremble, 315, 2258.
Daunse, 1024.
Daunsyng, 47.
*Dawed (=dowed), availed, profited, 1805.
Daylyeden, dallied, 1114.
Daynté, 121, 1250.
Debate, 68.
Debetande, debating, 2179.
*Debonerte, good manners, politeness.
*Dece,)
Des,) dais or table of state, 61,
Dese,) 75, 222, 250.
Defence, caution, 1282.
Defende, forbidden, 1156.
Dele, to deal (a blow), 295, 560; to give, bestow, 1085, 2192; to partake, 1968.
Dele, the devil, 2188.
Delen, (*pres. pl.*) deal, 1266.
Deles, deals, 397.
Delful, doleful, 560.
Deliuer, active, nimble, 2343.
Deliuerly, quickly, 2009.
Delyuer, 851.
Demay, dismay, 470.
*Deme, to judge, deem, 246, 1322, 2183.
Demed, esteemed, judged, determined, 240, 1089, 1668.
Demen (*pres. pl.*) judge, think fit, 1082, 1529.

Denaye, deny, refuse, 1497.
Denayed, refused, 1493.
Deneȝ, Danish, 2223.
Depaynt,) deposited, 620, 647.
Depaynted,)
Departed, severed, divided, 1335.
Deprece, release, 1219.
Depreced,) vanquished, bore down,
Depresed,) 6, 1770.
Dere, deer, beasts of chace, 1151, 1322.
Dere, joyful, delightful, 92, 1012, 1026, 1047; worthy, 47; precious, costly, 75, 121, 193, 571. Used substantively=worthy, noble, honourable (one), 678, 928.
*Dere, hurtful, injurious, 564.
Dered, injured, 1460.
Derely, joyfully, honourably, 817, 1031, 1253, 1327, 1559.
*Derf, strong, stern, severe, active, 564, 1000, 1233, 1492.
*Derfly,) quickly, suddenly,
Deruely,) firmly, 1183, 2834.
*Derne, secret, privy, 1012, 1047.
Dernly, secretly, silently, 1188, 2334. Should we not read *deruly*, *i.e.*, quickly, smartly?
Derrest, noblest, 445, 483.
*Derue=derf, strong, great, 558.
Derworthly, honourably, 114.
Destines, 564.
Destyne, 996.
Deve, to confound, 1286. Sc. *deve*, to confound, stupefy.
Deuise, 92.
Deuys, 617.
Dew, 519.
Deȝe, die, 996.
Diamaunteȝ, diamonds, 617.
Digne,) worthy, 1316.
Dyngne,)
*Dille, dull, foolish, 1529.
Disceuer, discover, 1862.
Discrye, describe, 81.
Diskouere, 418.
Dismay, 336.

Display, 955.
Displese, 2439.
Dispoyle, undress, 860.
Disserue, deserve, 452.
Disstrye3, destroys, 2375.
*Dit, fastened, 1233.
*Di3t, pronounce, make, 295; pre-
  pared, dressed, placed, made
  ready, 114, 678, 994, 1559,
  1884, 1223, 1689.
Do, place, lay, 1492; "*dos her
  forth*" = goes out, 1308; *dos*
  (*imp.*), do thou, 1533.
*Doel, ⎫
Dole, ⎭ sorrow, torment, 558.
Dok, tail, 193. O.N. *dockr.*
*Dole, part, 719.
*Dom, ⎫ judgment, sentence, 295,
Dome, ⎭   1216, 1968.
Donkande, moistening, damp; from
  donk, dank, moist, wet.
Doser, back of a seat, 478.
*Doted, became foolish, demented,
  1151, 1956.
Dot3, does, 2211.
Double, ⎫
Doubble, ⎭ 61, 483.
Doute, fear, 246, 442.
Douteles, 725.
*Douth, ⎫ people, nobles, 61, 1365,
Douthe, ⎭   1415, 1956.
Dowelle, dwell, 566.
Draueled, slumbered fitfully, 1750.
  A.S. *dréfan,* to disturb, trouble.
  "Of *dreflyng* and dremys quhat dow
     (avails) it to endite?"
          (G. Douglas, vol. i., p. 447.)
Dra3e3, draws, 1031.
Dra3t, drawbridge, 817.
Drechch, trouble, hurt (*not* delay, as
  Sir F. Madden suggests), 1972.
  A.S. *drécan,* to trouble, vex,
  oppress. See Glossary to Ham-
  pole.
Dredles, void of dread, 2334.
*Dreped, put to death, 725.
Dres, to prepare, go, 474.

Dressed, placed, set, 75, 2033;
  went, rose, 1415, 2009.
Dresses, ⎫ prepares, rises, 417, 445,
Dresse3, ⎭   566.
*Dre3, fierce, bold, 1750; used ad-
  verbially, 2263.
*Dre3ly, vigorously, 1026.
Driuande, driving, advancing
  quickly, 222.
Drof, drove, rushed, passed, 786,
  1151, 1176.
Dronken (*pret. pl.*) drank, 1025,
  1668.
Drope, 519.
Drouping, ⎫ uneasy, fitful slumber,
Drowping, ⎭ 1748, 1750. We often
  meet in O. E. works with the
  phrase "to *drowpe* and dare" =
  to be troubled and affrighted.
  O.N. *driúpr,* troubled. See *Drove*
  in Glossary to "Alliterative
  Poems."
Dro3, ⎫ drew, 1188, 1463.
Dro3en, ⎭
Dro3t = drought, dryness, 523.
*Drury, ⎫ amour, love, love-token,
Drwrye, ⎭   1507, 1517, 1805,
  2033, 2449.
*Dry3e, endure, suffer, 202, 560.
*Dry3e, stern, immovable, 335;
  enduring, tough, 724, 1460.
*Dry3tyn, the Lord, 724, 996, 1548.
*Dubbed, ornamented, dressed,
  clad, 75, 193, 571.
Dublet, 571.
*Dulful, doleful, grievous, 1517.
*Dunt, ⎫ blow, *dint,* 452, 1286.
Dunte, ⎭
Dust, 523.
Dut, mirth (?), 1020.
Dut, ⎫ doubted, feared, 222, 784,
Dutte, ⎭   2257.
Du3ty (= doughty), 724.
*Dyn, noise, revelry, 47.
Dynne3 (= dynge3 ?), strikes, 2105
*Dynt, blow, stroke, 315, 560,
  2105.

Dynte3, } blows, 336, 202, 1460.
Dyntte3, }
Dy3t. See *Di3t.*

Efte, afterwards, 641, 700, 788, 2388.
Eft-sone3, } forthwith, there-
Efter-sone3, } after, 1640, 2417.
*Egge, edge, 212. Used for the axe itself, 2392.
Eindele3 (=endele3), 629.
Eke, also, 90.
Elbowe, 184.
*Elde, age, 844, 1520.
Elle3, if that, 295.
Em, } uncle, 356, 543. A.S *eam.*
Eme, }
*Enbaned, supported (?), 790.
Enbelyse, to embellish, 1034.
Enbrauded, } embroidered, adorn-
Enbrawded, } ed, 78, 166, 606,
Enbrawden, } 856.
Enclyne, 340.
Endite, put (to death), 1600.
Enesed, entangled, clotted (?), 184. Sir F. Madden suggests *covered.* We might read *euesed*=bordered, from A.S. *efese,* rim, border.
Enfoubled, wrapt up, 959.
Enker, bright (applied to colour), 150, 2477. The same root enters into O.E. and Sc. *enkerly,* quickly, vigorously.
*Ennourned, } adorned, 634, 2027.
Ennurned, }
Enquest, inquiry, 1056.
Entayled, interwoven, embroidered, 612.
Enterlude3, 472.
Entyse, acquire, 2436.
Er, ere, before, previously, 92, 197, 712.
Erber, the conduit leading to the stomach; a hunting term, 1330.
*Erd, } earth, 27, 140, 881.
Erde, }
*Erde3, lands, 1808.

Erly, 567.
*Ernd, } errand, 257, 559, 809.
Ernde, }
Ermyn, 881.
Etayn, giant, 140. A.S. *eóten,* a giant, monster.
Etayne3, giants, 723.
Ethe, ask, 379, 2467.
Ethe, easy, 676.
Ette, ate, 113.
Euenden, evenly (?), perpendicularly (?), 1345.
Euensong, 932.
Eue3, borders, *eaves,* 1178. A.S. *efese,* brim, bank.
Expoun (=expound), describe, explain, 209, 1506.

Fade, hostile, 149. Isl. *fæd*=feud, enmity. S. Saxon, *ifæied.* O.E. *ivet.*
Fale, fallow (?), grassy (?), 728.
Falle, befall, happen, 483.
Falled, belonged, appertained, 2243.
Falle3, befalls, appertains, 1303, 1358, 2327.
Faltered, 430.
*Fange, take, receive, 391.
*Fannand, waving, flowing, 181.
Fantoum, phantom, illusion, 240.
*Farand, goodly, 101.
Fare, unusual display, entertainment, 537; behaviour, conduct, 1116, 2386; course, path, way, 694, 1703, 1793; proceeding, adventure, 2494; business, 409.
Faren, gone, 1231.
*Fare3, goes, journeys, 699; (*imp.*) go ye, 2149.
Faut, fault, 1551, 2435.
Fautles, } faultless, 640, 1761.
Fautle3, }
Fawne, to caress, 1919.
Fawty, faulty, 2382, 2886.
*Fax, } hair, 181.
Faxe, }

Fayly, to fail, 1067.

Fayle?, fails, 278, 455.

Fayn, glad, joyful, 388, 840, 1067.

Fayntyse, deceit, cowardice, 2435.
　O. Fr. *feintise, faintise,* from *feindre, faindre.*

Fayry?e, enchantment, magic, 240.
　"It was of *fayry,* as the people semed."
　　(Chaucer's Squyeres Tale.)

Faythely, certainly, 1636.

Feble, 354.

Feersly, 329.

Fee?, 1622.

Fela?es, fellows, 1702.

Fela?schyp, fellowship, 652.

Felde, fold, embrace, 841, 890.
　Cf. *feme* = foam.

*Fele,) many, 122, 239, 428,
Felle,) 1566.

Fele-fold, manifold, 1545.

Fele-kyn, many kinds of, 890.

Feler, more, greater, 1391.

Felle, hill, moor, 723. O.N. *fiall.*

Felle, befell, 1588.

Felle, skin, hide, 943, 1359, 1944.

*Felle, fierce, bold, furious, 291,
　847, 874. Used substantively,
　1585.

Fellely,) fiercely, cruelly, boldly,
Felly,) 2302.

Felle?, skins, 880, 1737.

Femed, foamed, 1572.

*Ferde, fear, 2130, 2272.

Ferde, ferden = proceeded, acted,
　149, 703, 1282, 1433. See *Fare.*

Ferde, feared, afraid, 1295, 1588,
　2382.

Fere, undaunted; literally, whole,
　sound, 103. Dan. *för.* O.N. *fœrr.*

*Fere, a companion, 676, 695, 915,
　2411; *in-fere* = together, in com-
　pany, 267.

Fere?, companions, 594.

*Ferk, to proceed, ride, 1072, 1973.

Ferked, ran, 2173.

*Ferke?,) rides, rises, 173, 2013.
Ferkke?,)

*Ferly, wonder, marvel, 716, 2414.

Ferly,) wondrous, wondrously,
Ferlyly,) 388, 741, 766, 1694,
　2494.

Ferlyes, marvels, 23.

Fermysoun, a hunting term, ap-
　plied to the time in which the
　male deer were *closed,* or not
　allowed to be killed, 1156.

Ferre, afar, 1093.

Fersly, brightly, 832.

Ferum, afar. See *On-ferum.*

Fest, secured, fastened, 2347.

Festned, fastened, 1783.

Feted, behaved, acted, 1282.

*Fetled, joined, 656.

Fetly, featly, 1758.

Fette, fetched, brought, 1084.

Fetures, 145.

Feye, dead, 1067. Sc. *fey.* Icel.
　feigr, fated.

Fe?t, fight, 717.

Fe?tyng, fighting, 267.

*Fildore, gold thread, 189.

Fire = fere (?) = fear, 1304.

Firre,) further, moreover, 378,
Fyrre,) 411, 1105, 2121.

First, early, youthful, 54.

Flat, ground, field, 507.

Fla?,) flew, fled, 459, 2274,
Fla?e,) 2276.

Flet,) floor (originally applied
Flette,) to the *hall* itself. See
　Romance of Alexander, ed. Ste-
　venson, l. 821), 294, 568, 832,
　859, 1374, 1653, 1925. A.S.
　flett.

*Flete, fletted, flew, 1566.

Flone, arrow, 1161. A.S. *flán.*

Flone?, arrows, 1566.

Flosche, flood, pool, marsh, 1430.
　O.Sc. *flouss.* "Plasche or *flasche,*
　where reyne watyr stondythe,
　torrens, lacuna." (Prompt.
　Parv.)

Floten, removed, 714.

Flynt, 459.

Fly3e, fly, 524.

Fly3es, flies, 166.

Fnast, to breathe hard, 1587. A.S. *fnæst*, a puff, blast.

Fnasted, breathed hard, 1702.

Foch, fetch, 396.

Fochche3, fetches, 1961.

*Fold, } earth, 23, 196, 396, 422.
Folde, }

Folden, folded, 959; plighted, 1783.

Folde3 (*imp.*), grant thou, 359; (*pres.*) accords, 499.

Fole, foal, 173, 459.

Fole, fool, 1545.

Foly, foolishly, 324.

Fol3ande = following, suitable, 145, 859.

Fol3ed, followed, 1895.

Fol3es, follows, 1164.

*Fonde, to try, endeavour, 291, 565, 986; might find, 1875.

Fondet, } attempted, proved,
Founded, } 1549, 2125, 2130.

*Fonge, to take, receive, 816, 1556, 1622; (*pret.*) 646, 1315, 1363.

Fonge, } (*p.p.*) taken, 919, 1315.
Fonged, }

Fongen, took, 1265.

Foo = Northumbrian *fa*, bad, vile, hence rugged, rough, 1430, 2326. A.S. *fáh*, hostile. Sir F. Madden suggests *large, largely*. In the *Cursor Mundi*, fol. 48, *fa* is applied to clothing. In the *Morte Arthure*, ed. Halliwell, p. 63, we have the phrase "*fawe* ythe3," the rough waves.

"The pryce schippez of the porte provene theire depnesse
And fondez wyth ful saile ower the *fawe* ythez."

For, because, 258; before (?), 965, 1822.

For-be = for-by, surpassing, 652.

Forde3, fords, 699.

Forfaren, destroyed, 1895.

*Forferde, destroyed, killed, 1617.

Forlancyng, cutting off, 1334.

Forlonde3, 699.

*Forme, beginning, 499; foremost, 2373.

Forne, formerly (?), 2422.

For-olde, became very old, 1440.

Forsake, to deny, 475.

Forsness, vigour, strength, 646.

Forsoke, denied, 1826.

*Forst, frost, 1694.

*Forth, } passage, ford, stream,
Forthe, } 1585, 1617, 2173.
For3, }

*For-thi, } therefore, 27, 240, 283,
For-thy, } 455.

*Forward, } covenant, 1105, 1395,
Forwarde, } 1636.

Forwarde3 (*pl.*), covenants, 378, 409, 1405.

For-wondred, astonished, 1660.

For3ate, forgot, 1472.

For-3elde, requite, 839, 1279, 1535. See *3elde*.

Fote3, feet, 574.

Fotte, fetch, 451.

Founded, came, 267.

*Founde3, goes, 1585, 2229.

Fourche3, a hunting term, applied to the *forks* or *haunches* of the deer, 1357.

"And after the ragge-boon kytteth euyn also,
The *forchis* and the sydes euyn bytwene,
And loke that your knyues ay whettyd bene;
Thenue turne vp the *forchis*, and frote theym wyth blood,
For to saue grece; so deo men of good."
(Boke of St. Alban's, 1496.)

Foyned, turned aside, 428.

*Foysoun, plenty, 122.

*Fraist, } to ask, seek, 409; (1*st*
Frayste, } *pers. sing.*) 279.

Frayst, } asked, 324, 391, 1395;
Fraysted, } tried, proved, 1679.

Fraysteჴ, askest, 455; tries, 503.

Fraunchis, } frankness, liberality,
Fraunchyse, } 652, 1264.

*Frayn, to seek, 489.

Frayned, asked, 359, 703, 1046.

*Fre, noble, 101, 847, 1156, 1885, 1961. Used substantively, 1545, 1549, 1783.

*Freke, man, warrior, 149, 196, 241, 651.

Frekes, }
Frekeჴ, } men, 703, 840, 1172.

Frekeჴ, man's, 537.

Frely, noble, 816, 894.

Fremedly, as a stranger, 714. A.S. *fremed*, foreign, alien, strange.

Frenges, fringes, 598.

Frenkysch, French (?), frank (?), jocular (?), 1116. Does not *frenkysch fare* = extraordinary conduct?

"In faith, Noe, I had as leif thou had sleped, for all thy *frankish fare*, For I will not doe after thy red."
(Chester Mysteries.)

Fres, froze, 728.

Fresche (meat), 122.

Freschly, quickly, 1294.

*Frithe, } an enclosed wood, 1430,
Frythe, } 1973, 2151.

Frytheჴ, woods, 695.

*Fro, from (the time that), 8, 62; from, 1336.

Frote, rub, 1919.

Frounses, wrinkles, contracts, 2306.

Frount, forehead, 959.

*Fulsun (=fulsen), to help, aid, 99. A.S. *fulstan*, to help.

Funde, }
Funden, } found, 396, 640.

Furred, 1737.

Fust, fist, hand, 391.

Fute, } (=feut) track of a fox or
Fuyt, } beast of chace by the odour, 1425. "*Fewte*, vestigium." (Prompt. Parv.)

Fych, fix, 396.

Fyched, fixed, 658.

Fyked, shrank, was troubled, 2274.

Fyled, ground, 2225.

*Fylyoleჴ, round towers, 796.

Fylle, fulfil, 1405, 1934.

Fylor, grindstone (?), 2225.

*Fylter, contend, join in contest, 986.

Fynde=fyned=ended (?), 660.

Fyne, perfect, unconditional, 1239.

Fynisment, end, finish, 499.

Fynly, wholly (?), 1391.

Fyrre, moreover, 2121.

Fyskeჴ, runs, 1704. A.S. *fysian*, *fysan*, to hasten, rush.

Fyჴed, were fair (?), 796. A.S. *fægr*, fair. Does *fyჴed* = united, extended, from A.S. *gefeg*, union?

*Game, }
Gamen, } sport, game, 365.

Gamnes, }
Gamneჴ, } games, sports, 1319.

*Gart, caused, 2460.

Gargulun, part of the inwards of a deer, apparently included in the *numbles*, 1335, 1340.

Garysoun (=warisoun), treasure, reward, 1225, 1807, 1837. Fr. *garison*.

Garyteჴ, watch towers, 791.

Gast=aghast, afraid, 325.

Gate, way, road, path, 696, 778, 930.

Gates, roads, ways, 709.

Gaudi = gaude (?) = ornament (?), 167.

Gay, } an epithet used substan-
Gaye, } tively, and applied to both sexes, 970, 1215, 1822, 2035.

Gayly, 598.

*Gayn, to befit, 584.

Gayn, serviceable, 178; fit, proper, 1241.

Gayn, promptly, quickly, 1621.

Gaynest, nearest, speediest, 1973.

Gaynly, fitly, promptly, 476,1297.

Gederes, gathers, 421, 777.

Gef, gave, 370, 668, 2349.

Gentyle, pleasant, 1022.

*Gere, armour, 569, 584.

Gered, arrayed, dressed, 86, 179, 957, 2227; disposed, 791; made, fashioned, 1832.

Gere3, apparel, 1470.

*Gere3, vb. arrays, 1872.

Geserne,) axe, 288, 326, 375,
Giserne,) 2265. O.Fr. gisarme.

Get, booty, gain, 1638.

Geten, got, 1171, 1625.

Gif, to give, 288, 365.

Glade, to gladden, 989.

Gladloker, gladlier, 1064.

*Glam, talk, conversation, clamour, 1426, 1652.

*Glauerande, noisy, yelping, 1426.

Glaumande, noisy, riotous, 46. See Glam.

Gle, 46.

Glede, burning coal, ember, 1609. A.S. gléd.

Gleme, 598.

Glemered, glimmered, gleamed, 172.

*Glent, glance, 1290.

*Glent, glanced, looked, 82, 476; shone, 172, 569, 604; brightened, started up, 1652; shrank, 2290.

Glod = glided, came, 661.

Glode = clod (?), clump, hillock, tuft (?), 2266.

Glodes, pl. of Glode, 2181.

Gloue3, 583.

*Glyfte, looked, 2265.

"Sir Gawayne glyftes on the gome with a glade wille."

(Morte Arthure, p. 211.)

*Gly3t, looked, 842, 970.

Goande, walking, 2214.

Godly,   ) goodly, courteously,
Goudly,   ) 273, 584, 1933.
Godlych,)

Gog, a corruption of God, 390.

*Gomen, game, sport, 273, 661, 1014, 1376.

Gomenly, playfully, 1079.

*Gomnes,) games, 495, 683, 1894.
Gomne3,)

*Gopnyng = glopnyng = affright.

*Gorde, p.p. gird, 1851.

Gorde3, strikes, spurs, 2062.

Gorger = gorget, wrapper or covering for the throat, 957.

Gost, spirit, life, 2250.

Gostlych, ghostly, 2461.

Got3, goes, 375, 1293; (imp.) 2119.

Goule3,) gules, 619, 663. O.Fr.
Gowle3,) gule.

Gracons = gracous = gracious, fair, beautiful, 216.

Grant-merci,) gramercy, thanks,
Graunt-mercy,) 838, 1037, 1392.

Grattest, greatest, 207, 1441.

Gray, adj. 82.

Grayes, becomes gray, 527.

Grayn, 211.

*Grayth,) ready, prepared, prompt,
Graythe,) 448, 597, 2047.

Graythed, arrayed, dressed, prepared, 74, 109, 666, 876, 2259.

Graythely, readily, speedily, 417, 876, 1006, 1335; willingly, 1470; steadfastly, firmly, 2292.

*Graythe3, makes ready, goes, 2014.

Grece, 425.

*Grem,) anger, 312, 2370; mis-
Greme,) chief, 2251; displeasing, 1507.

Grenne = grin, make game, 464; A.S. grennian.

Gres, 1326.

Gres,   ) grass, 235, 2181.
Gresse,)

Gret, greeted, accosted, 842, 1933.

Grete = great (ones), 2490.

Grete, cry, weep, 2157. A.S. grætan.

Greue, grove, copse, 1355, 1707, 1898, 1974.

Greues, }
Greue}, } groves, 207, 508.

Greue}, greaves, leg-armour, 575.

Grome (=groom), man, knight, 1006.

Gronyed, grunted as a wild boar. A.S. *grunan*, to grunt.

*Gruchyng, displeasing, misliking, 2126.

*Grwe=gre, will, 2251.

Gryed, trembled, was troubled, agitated, 2370. A.S. *grýre*, horror, terror.

*Grymme, sharp, 413; cruel, 2260.

*Gryndel, angry, wroth, fierce, 2338.

Gryndel-layk, anger, fierceness, 312.

Gryndelly, wrathfully, 2299.

Gryndelston, grindstone, 2202.

Gryped, grasped, 421, 1335.

Gurd, gird, 588.

Gyld, gilded, 569.

*Gyng, assembly, 224.

*Gyrde}, strikes, spurs, 2160.

Haboe, }
Habbes, } have, hast, 327, 452, 626, 1252.
Habbe}, }

Hadet=halet (?)=haled (?), 681. See *Haled*.

Halawed, hallowed, 1723.

*Halce=halse, neck, 427.

Halched, embraced, 939; looped, fastened, 185, 218, 657, 1852.

Halche}, fastens, 1613.

Halde, to hold, 1125.

Halden, held, 124; obliged, bound, 1040, 1828; esteemed, 1297.

Haldes, } holds, 53, 627; journeys,
Halde}, } 698.

*Haled, rushed, 458; rose, 788; pulled, hauled, 1338; shot, discharged, 1455; trimmed, 157; gone, 1049.

Hales, drives, rushes, 136.

Half, behalf, 2149.

Halidaye}, festivals, 1049.

Halme, handle, 218, 330, 2224.

Halowyng, 1602.

*Hals, }
Halse, } neck, 621, 1353, 1639.

Halt, held, 2079.

Halue, behalf, 326, 692, 2119; side, 742, 1552; sides, 2070, 2165.

Halydam, reliques of the saints (?), or the sacrament (?), 2123.

*Hal}es, saints, 2122.

Hamloune}, crosses, winds, a hunting term, used of the wiles of the fox, 1708.

Han, (*pl.*) have, 23, 1089, 2093.

Hanselle, specimen, first occurrence, 491. O.N. *handsel*, stipulatio manufactu.

*Hap, fortune, 48; "*hap vpon he}e*" =good fortune every where. Sir F. Madden thinks that it is somewhat equivalent to *haphazard*.

Hapnest, most fortunate, 56.

*Happe, cover, enclose, 1224.

Happed, fastened, 655; wrapped, 864.

Hardi, } 59, 371.
Hardy, }

Harled, drawn, trailed, 744. See *Haled*.

Harnays, 590.

Harnayst, 592.

Hasel, 744.

Haspe, chain, fastening, 1233.

*Hasped, clasped, closed, 281, 590, 831.

*Hasppe}, clasps, 1388.

Hastlette}, part of the inwards of a wild boar, 1612. In modern writers it is spelt *harslets, haslets*.

*Hat, } am named, 253, 381, 2445;
Hatte, } is called, 10.

*Hathel, an adjective used substantively to denote a noble person, knight or warrior, 221, 234,

Heʒ, } high, 48, 222, 593; noble,
Heʒe, }   812, 831 ; important,
1051 ; used adverbially, 1417.

Heʒly, devoutly, 755, 773 ; highly,
greatly, 949; quickly, 983. A.S.
hige, careful, diligent.

Heʒt, height, 788.

Hider, hither, 264.

Hiʒed, hastened, 826, 1152. See
Hyʒ.

Hit, it, joined to a plural noun,
280, 1251.

Hiʒe, } noble, 120; loud, 307, 468,
Hyʒe, }   1165, 1602 ; tall, 1154 ;
used substantively for heights,
high grounds, 1152, 1169, 2004.

Hiʒlich, noble, admirable, 183.

Hiʒtly, fitly, 1612. A.S. *hyhtlive,*
gladly, diligently.

Ho, she, 934, 948, 1001.

Hod, } hood, 155, 2297.
Hode, }

Hoge, huge, 208, 743.

Hol, } whole, entire, 1338, 1406,
Hole, }   1613, 2296.
Holle, }

*Holde, castle, mansion, 771.

Holde, faithfully, 2129. A.S. *held.*
Germ. *hold.*

Holdely, faithfully, carefully, 1875,
2016.

Holly, wholly, 1049, 1257.

Holsumly, comfortably, 1731.

*Holt, } forest, 742, 1677, 1697.
Holte, }

Holteʒ, forests, 1320.

Holyn-bobbe, holly-bough, 206.

Holʒ, hollow, 2182.

Hom, them, 99, 819, 979, 984.

Homered, hammered, struck, 2311.

Homes, abodes, dwellings, 12.

Honde-selle, gift, 66. See *Hanselle.*

Hondele, handle, use, 289.

Hone, delay, 1285.

Hoo, stop, 2330.

Hope, think, trust, 140, 352, 395,
2301.

Hor, their, 130, 1014, 1127, 1139.

Hore, hoary, 743.

Hose, 157.

Hostel, dwelling, inn, 805. O.Fr.
hosteil.

*Houed, tarred, 785, 2168.

Houes, hoofs, 459.

Hoʒes, houghs, 1357. A.S. *hoh.*

Hult, hilt, 1594.

Hunt, hunter, huntsman, 1422,
1701.

Huntes, hunters, 1147, 1604, 1910.

Hwe, *hue,* colour, complexion, 147,
234.

Hwen, hew, cut, 1346.

Hwes, } hues, 707, 867, 1738.
Hweʒ, }

Hyghe! } a shout or exclamation
Hyʒe! } of the hunters, 1445.

Hyʒ, *sb.* high, 302.

Hyʒ, *vb.* hasten, 299, 2121.

Hyʒ, *sb.* haste, 245.

Hyʒe, noble, etc. See *Hiʒe.*

Hyʒen, hasten, 1910.

Hyʒes, } hastens, 521, 1351, 1462.
Hyʒeʒ, }

*Hyʒt, promised, 1966, 2218.

Hyʒt, height, stature, 332.

Iche, each, 126, 1811.

Ile, 7, 698.

Ilk, } same, 24, 1062, 1256,
Ilke, }   1385.

*Ilyche, alike, 44.

Innogh,
Innoghe, } enough, 77, 219, 404,
Inoʒ, }   514, 1401, 1948.
Inoʒe,
Innowe,

Inwyth, within, 1055.

*Irked, were fatigued, tired, 1573.

*I-wis, } truly, certainly, 252,
I-wyis, } 264, 1035, 1065, 1226,
I-wysse, } 1230, 1276, 1487.

*Iapeʒ, jokes, jests, 542, 1957.

Ientyle, gentle, of noble birth or
breeding, 542.

Ioly, 86.
Iolyly, gaily, 42.
Ioparde, 97.
Icytnes, youth, 86.
Iusted, 42.
Iustyng, 97.

*Kachande, catching, reining up, 1581.
Kanel, collar, neck, 2298.
Kauelacioun, strife, 2275. See *Caueloun₃.*
Kay, left, 422. O.Dan. *kay, kei.*
*Kayre, to journey, depart, 1048, 1670.
Kayred, turned, returned, 43.
*Ka₃t,) took, received, 643,
Ka₃ten,) 1118
*Kende = kenned, taught, 1489.
Kene, bold, brave, 321; active, 482.
Kenel, 1140.
Kenet, hound, 1701.
Kenly, quickly, 1048.
Kenne=bikenne=commend, 2067.
*Kennes, teaches, 1484.
Kepe, care, heed, 546.
Kepe, to heed, or meet in a hostile way, 307; take heed, 372.
Kerchofes, kerchiefs, covering for the head, 954.
Kerre, rock, 1431. A.S. *carr.*
*Kest, chance, blow (?), 2298; twist, knot, 2376; stratagem, 2413.
Kest, raised, 64; cast, 228, 1192, 1355; thought, formed a plan, 1855; set, appointed, 2242.
Kesten, cast, 1649.
*Keuer, to arrive, accomplish, 750, 804; gain, 1221, 1254; recover, 2298.
Keuered, recovered, 1755.
Keuere₃, obtains, brings, 1539; descends, 2221.
Knaged, nailed, riveted, 577. Sw. *nagga,* to prick.
Knape, a man, 2136. A.S. *cnapa.*

Knarre, rock, cliff, 1434. Dan. *knort,* a *knur,* knob.
Knarre₃=rocks, 721, 2166.
Knawen, know, 133.
Knitten, joined, 1331.
Knokled, with craggy projections, rugged, 2166. Du. *knoke,* a knot in a tree. Ger. *knochel,* a *knuckle,* knot.
Knorned, rugged, 2166. Sw *knorla,* to twist, curl.
Knot, a hunting term, borrowed from and used as the French *nœud,* 1334.
Knot, crag, 1431, 1434.
Knote₃, knobs, rivets, 577.
Knotte, 188, 194.
Knyt, made, 1642.
*Koyntyse, cunning, 2447.
Kowarde, 2131.
*Kyd,) known, renowned, 51,
Kydde,) 263, 1520; directed, 775; shewed, manifested, 2340.
Kyn, kind, 890.
Kynnes, kinds, 1886.
Kynde, lineage, race, 5; nature, disposition, reason, 321, 1348.
Kynde, suitable, 473.
Kyndely, suitably, 135.
Kyrf, cut, blow, 372. A.S. *cyrf.*
Kyrk, church, 2196.
*Kyrtel, tunic, gown, 1831.
*Kyth,) country, land, territory,
Kythe,) kingdom, 460, 2120.

*Lach, to take, receive, accept, 234, 292, 1502, 1676.
Lachen (*pl.*) take, 1027, 1131.
Laches,) takes, receives, 595,
Lache₃,) 936, 1029.
Lachche₃,)
Lachet, clasp, tie, 591.
Lad, led, 947.
Ladé, lady, 1810.
Laft (=left), granted, delivered, 369.

Lag=lagh=law=low (?), 1729.

Laght. See *Laȝt*.

*Lance,) ride forth (?), 1175 ; tell,
Launce,)   2124.

Lanced, rode, 1561 ; uttered, threw
out, 1766, 1212.

Lancen, fall quickly, drop off, 526.

Langaberde, Lombards, 12.

Lante, lent, gave, 2250.

*Lappe, lappet, hem, 936.

Lapped, wrapped, folded, 217, 575.

*Lappeȝ, embraces, 973.

Lappeȝ, flaps, 1350.

Larges,) liberality, 2381 ; large-
Largesse,)   ness, 1627.

Lasse, less, 87.

Lassen, to lessen, 1800.

*Lathe, injury, harm, 2507.

*Lathed, invited, 2403. Sir F.
Madden says it is "perhaps a
form of *laȝed*, laughed."

Launced. See *Lanced*.

*Launde, clear level space in a
wood, plain, lawn, 765, 2146,
2154, 2174, 2333.

Lausen, to loose, 1784.

*Lawe, mount, hill, 765, 2171,
2175.

Lawe, manner (?), 790.

Lawseȝ, looses, 2376.

*Layk, sport, game, 1023, 1125,
1513.

Layke, to sport, play, 1111.

Layked, sported, played, 1554,
1560.

Laykeȝ, *sb*. sports, 262.

Laykeȝ, *vb*. plays, sports, 1178.

Laykyng, sport, playing, 472.

*Layne, to conceal, keep secret,
1863, 2124, 2128 ; (*imp.*) 1786.

Layt, lightning, 199.

*Layt, to look, seek, 411, 449.

Laytes, seeks, 355.

Laȝande, laughing, 988, 1068, 1212.

Laȝe,) laugh, 472, 464, 2514.
Laȝen,)

Laȝed, laughed, 69, 909, 1079.

Laȝes,) laughs, 316, 1479.
Laȝeȝ,)

Laȝt, took, caught, received, 328,
433, 667, 1830, 2449 ; taken,
received, 156, 971, 2507 ; caught,
433.

Laȝter, laugh, laughter, 1217.

Laȝyng, laughing, 1954.

Le,) *lea*, land, plain, 849, 1893.
Lee,)

Ledande, leading, 1894.

*Lede, man, person, 98, 540, 1063,
1195, 2095 ; people, folk, 258 ;
land, territory, 833, 1113.

Ledeȝ, men, 38, 126, 679, 1231.

*Lef, dear, agreeable, 909, 1111,
1924.

Legge, liege, 346.

Leke, fastened, encircled, 1830.
O.Sw. *lycka*.

Lel,) loyal, faithful, 35, 1513,
Lele,)   1516.

Lelely, loyally, faithfully, 449,
1863, 2124.

*Lemand,) gleaming, shining,
Lemande,)   485, 1119.

Lemed, shone, gleamed, 591, 1137,
2010.

Lemman, mistress, 1781. A. S.
leof-man.

*Lende, to dwell, tarry, continue,
1100, 1499.

*Leng,) to dwell, tarry, remain,
Lenge,)   411, 254, 1068.

Lenge, long, 88.

Lenged, dwelt, tarried, 1194, 1299.
1683.

Lenges,) dwells, tarries, 536, 693.
Lengeȝ,)

*Lent, remained, sate, was sta-
tioned, 1002, 2440 ; occupied,
1319. See *Lende*.

Lenthe, length, 1231.

Lentoun, Lent, 502.

*Lere, countenance, 318, 418.

*Lere, loss, 1109 ; "*lere other better*"
="loss or gain." Sir F. Madden

suggests "to teach" as the rendering of *lere*.

*Lese, to lose, 2142.

Lested, lasted, 805.

Let, caused, 1084; "*let not*," was not able, 1733.

Lete, to look, 1206; appeared, 1281; feigned, acted, 1190, 1201, 2257. A.S. *lætan*, to pretend.

*Lothe, to depress, moderate, 2438.

Lether, skin, 1360.

Lette, hindrance, 2142.

Lette, to stop, tarry, 2303.

Letted, hindered, 1672.

Lette₃ (be), leave off, 1840.

Lettrure, science, 1513.

*Leude,) man, knight, 133, 232,
Lude,   )   449, 675, 851, 908,
1109; territory, land, 1124.

Leudes, man's, 2449.

Leude₃, men, 849, 1023, 1413. See *Lede*.

Leudle₃, companionless, 693.

Leue, live, 1035.

Leue, believe, 2421, 1784, 2128.

*Leue, dear, beloved, 1133, 2054.

Leuer, rather, liefer, 1251; dearer, 1782.

Leuest, dearest, most precious, 49, 1802.

*Lewd,) ignorant,   unlearned,
Lewed,)   1528.

Lewte, loyalty, faith, 2366, 2381.

Le₃, lay, 2006.

Le₃ten, took, 1410. See *La₃t*.

Liflod, living, livelihood, 133.

Li₃te₃,) alights, 1906, 2176.
Ly₃te₃,)

Like, please, 87.

List, pleasure (?), 1719.

*Litherne₃, fierceness, 1627.

*Lode, guidance, 969; conduct, behaviour, 1284.

Lodly = loudly (?), 1634.

*Lodly, uncourteously, 1772.

Lofden (*pret. pl.*), loved, 21.

Loft,) chamber, 1096, 1676.
Lofte,)

Loke, preserve, 2239.

Loken, secured, fastened, enclosed, 35, 765, 2487.

Lokke₃, looks, 419.

*Lome, tool, axe, 2309.

Longed, belonged, appertained, 1524, 2515.

Longe₃, belongs, 2381.

Longynge, regret, trouble, 540.

Lopen, leapt, 1413.

Lore, learning, skill, 665.

Lortschyp, lordship, 849.

Los,) renown, famed, 258, 1528.
Lose,) Fr. *los*.

*Lote, sound, word, and hence noise, mirth, jest, 119, 1623, 1917, 2211.

*Lote, feature, aspect, gesture, 639.

*Lote₃, words, 988, 1086, 1116, 1399, 1954. Sir F. Madden thinks that *lote* is connected with French *losterie*, badinage.

Lothe, unwillingness, 127; loath, unwilling, 1578.

Louked, fastened, looped, 217.

Loukes,) locks, 628, 2007.
Lowke₃,)

Loupe, loop-hole in a castle, 792.

*Lout,) to bow down, bend to,
Loute,)   248.

Loutes,) descends,   833,   933;
Loute₃,) stoops,bends,1306,1504.

Louue, for *louie* (?), or loune (= *lovne*, praise, 1251.

Louelych, lovingly, 1410.

Loueloker, lovelier; used substantively = the fairer one, 973.

Louelokest, 52.

Louied, loved, 87, 702.

Louy, love, 1795.

Louyes,) loves, 2099, 2468.
Louies,)

*Lowande, shining, 236; conspicuous, 679, 868. Cf. O.E. *low*, a flame, light.

Lowe, quiet, secret, 1399.

Loʒ, } low, 302, 1040, 1170.
Loʒe, }

Loʒe, laughed, 2389.

Loʒly, lowly, humbly, 851, 1960.

Lude. See *Lede* and *Leude.*

Luf, love, pleasure, 1086, 1284, 1524.

Luf-laʒyng = luf-laughing = amorous play, 1777.

Lufly, } *adj* lovely, fair, comely,
Luflych, } agreeable, amiable, 38, 575, 792, 868, 981, 1469, 1480, 1657, 1757 ; *adv.* courteously, lovingly, becomingly, 254, 595, 1206, 1306, 1583.

Luflyly, courteously, lovingly, 369. 2176, 2514.

Lufsome, } lovely, 1814.
Lufsum, }

Luf-talkyng, 927.

Lur, loss, misfortune, 355, 1284, 1682.

Lurkkes, 1180.

*Lut, } *pret.* of *loute,* stooped, bowed
Lutte, } down, 418, 2236, 2255.

*Lyfte, sky, heaven, 1256.

Lyfte, left, 698, 947.

*Lygeʒ, lies, 1179.

*Lyk, } please, 390 ; pleased, 1281.
Lyke, }

Lykker-wys, more pleasing, delightful, 968.

*Lymp, to happen, befall, 1109.

Lymped, befell, 907.

Lyn, } *adj.* linen, 608.
Lyne, }

Lynde, wood, tree, 256, 2176.

Lynde-wodes, 1178.

Lyndes (=lendes), loins, 139. A.S. *lendenu,* loins.

Lyre, linen ; whence for female apparel in general, 1814.

Lyre, complexion, countenance, 943, 2228 ; skin, 2080.

Lyst, desired, willed, 941, 1784, 2049.

Lyste, pleases, 2133.

Lystily, } quickly, promptly,
Lystyly, } 1190, 1334.

*Lyte, few, 701, 1776.

*Lythen, to listen, 1719.

Lyʒe, to lie, recline, 1096, 1994.

Lyʒt, alighted, 1921.

Lyʒt, light, not heavy, 608.

Lyʒt, to descend, alight, fall, 423, 1175, 1373, 2220.

Lyʒteʒ, alights. See *Liʒteʒ.*

Lyʒten (*pl.*), alight, 526.

Lyʒtly, easily, 423, 1299.

Mach = match, to encounter, meet in combat, 282.

*Mace = mas = makes, 1885.

*Madde, rage with love, 2414.

Ma fay ! ma foi ! 1495.

Mas, } makes, 106.
Mase, }

Males, } bags, trunks, 1129, 1809.
Maleʒ, }

Malt, dissolved, melted, 2080.

Maner, 90.

Manereʒ, 924.

Manerly, 1656.

Mansed = manased, menaced, 2345.

*Marre, to destroy, 2262.

*Mat, } overcome, discouraged,
Mateʒ } wearied, 336, 1568

Matyneʒ, } morning prayers, 756,
Matynnes, } 2188.

*Maw-gref, in spite of, 1565.

*May, maiden, 1795.

*Mayn, great, powerful, strong, 94, 187, 336, 497.

Maynteines, maintains, 2053.

Maʒtyly, mightily, forcibly, 2262, 2290.

Me, used in apposition with the subject of the sentence = myself, thyself, etc., 1214, 1905, 1932, 2014, 2144.

*Mele, to speak, talk, 2295, 2503.

Meled, spoke, talked, 447, 1280, 2373.

Meleȝ, speak, 543, 974, 2336.
Melle,) conflict, battle, 342, 644,
Melly,) 1451.
*Mene, to signify, 232 ; devise,
 985 ; make attempt on (?), 1157.
*Menged, mixed, 1720.
*Mensk,) honour, worship, 834,
Menske,) 914, 2052 ; worship-
 ful, 964.
Mensked, honourably decked, 153.
Menskes, honours, 2410.
Menskful, honourable, 555, 1628,
 1809.
Menskly, honourably, 1312, 1983.
*Meny,) retinue, household, com-
Meyny,) pany, 101, 1372, 1625,
 1729, 2468.
Menyng, knowledge, remembrance,
 924.
Mere, simple, pure, good, 153,
 878, 924, 1495.
*Mere,) =meer, boundary, and
Merk,) hence appointed place
 of meeting, 1061, 1073.
Merkkeȝ, aims at, 1592.
Mes, mess, meal, 999.
Messes, 999.
Messe-quyle, the time of celebra-
 ting mass, 1097.
Metely, measurely, fitly, 1004,
 1414.
*Methles, uncourteous, without
 pity, 2106.
Meued, moved, 90.
Meȝel-mas, Michaelmas, 532.
Miche, much, 569.
Misy, quagmire, 749. Still used
 in the North.
Mo, more, 23, 730, 770.
Mode, mind, 1475.
Molaynes, round embossed orna-
 ments (?), 169.
*Molde, earth, ground, 137, 914,
 964.
Mon, used as the Germ. man, and
 Fr. on, for one, a person, 1209,
 1484.

Mon, must, 1811. O.N. mun.
More, greater, bigger, 649, 2100.
Moroun, morrow, 1208.
Morsel, 1690.
Mot, may, 342, 387, 2053 ; must,
 1965, 2510.
Mote=moot, assemblage, meeting,
 635, 910. A.S. mót.
*Mote, castle, 764, 2052.
Mote, atom, 2009.
Mote,) notes or measures of a
Moteȝ,) bugle, 1141, 1364.
Mounture, saddle horse, 1691.
Mournyng, 543.
Moȝt,) might, 84, 1871, 1953.
Moȝten,)
Much, great, loud, 182, 2336.
Much-quat = much-what, many
 matters, 1280.
Muckel, greatness (of stature, size),
 142.
Muged, was cloudy, 142. O.N.
 mugga, der nubilus. Sir F.
 Madden renders it stirred,
 hovered.
Mulne, mill, 2203. A.S. myln.
*Munt, blow, 2350. See Mgnt.
Munt, feigned, 2262.
Muryly, merrily, pleasantly, play-
 fully, 2336, 2345.
Mused, stood in doubt, 2424.
 " Mowsyn or priuely stodyyn
 (stondyn a dowt, K. stodyn a
 dowte, H. musen or stodien a
 doughte, P.) Muso, Musso."
 (Prompt. Parv.)
Mute, pack of hounds, 1451, 1720.
Mute=meet, meeting of hunters,
 1915. A.S. mút.
Muthe=mouthe, 447, 1428.
Mwe, to move, 1565.
Myd-morn, 1073.
Mynged, remarked, announced,
 1422. A.S. myngian, to inform,
 mark. Sir F. Madden suggests
 assembled as the meaning of
 mynged.

Myneȝ, calls to remembrance, 995.
*Mynne, to think, remember, devise, 141, 1681, 1800, 1992, 1769.
Mynne, less, 1881. O.N. *minni*.
Mynned, devised, 982.
Mynstralcie, 484.
*Mynt, aim, blow, 3345.
Myntes (*pl.*), blows, 2352.
Myntest, didst aim or strike, 2274.
*Mynteȝ, aims, strikes, 2290.
Myre, 749.
Mys-boden, offered wrong, 2339.
Mysses, faults, 2391.
Myst-hakel, cloak of mist, 2081.
   A.S. *hacele*, a cloak, mantle.
Myȝtes, powers, 282.

Nade, had not, 724, 763.
Naf, have not, 1066.
*Nakerys = nakers, drums, 1016.
*Nakryn (*gen. pl.*), of drums, 118.
Nar, are not, 2092.
Naunt, *thy naunt*, thine aunt, 2467.
Nauther,) neither, 203, 430, 1095.
Nawther,)
Nay, denied, refused, 1836.
Nayleȝ, 603.
Naylet, nailed, 599.
Nayted, celebrated, 65. O.E. *nayte*, to use, employ, enjoy. O.N. *neyta*. Left unexplained by Sir F. Madden.
Naȝt, night, 1407.
Nede,) of necessity, necessarily,
Nedes,) 1287, 1771, 1965, 2510.
Nedeȝ,)
*Negh,) to approach, 1054 ; to
Neghe,) touch, 1836. See *Neȝe*.
Neked, little or nothing, 1062, 1805.
*Neme, take, 1347.
Nerre, nearer, 237, 556, 1306.
*Neuen, to name, speak of, 58.
Neuened, named, mentioned, 65, 541.
Neuenes, names, 10.

Neȝ,)
Neȝe,) nigh, 929, 1771, 1922.
Nieȝ,)
*Neȝe, to approach, 1575.
Neȝed, approached, 132, 697, 929.
Neȝes, approaches, 1998.
Nif, unless, 1769.
Nikked naye, denied strongly, 706, 2471.
Nirt, cut, hurt, 2498.
Nobelay, nobleness, 91.
*No-bot, except, 2182.
Noghe = nyghe = nigh, 697.
Noke, corner, nook, 660.
Nolde, would not, 1054, 1825.
Nome, name, 10, 408, 937.
Nome, took, 809, 1407.
Nomen, taken, 91.
Noneȝ, nonce, 844.
*Norne,) to proffer, 1661, 1669,
Nurne,) 1823 ; allege, 2443.
*Note, occasion, business, use, 358, 599.
Note, throat-knot (?), (Fr. *nœud*) 420. But perhaps "*to the note*" = to the axe, *note* being of the same origin as the preceding word = a *tool, weapon*.
Note, noted (?), 2092.
Noumbles, parts of the inward of the deer, 1347.
*Nouthe,) now, 1251, 1934, 2466 ;
Nowthe,) not (?), 1784.
Nowther, neither, 659.
Nowel, Noel, Christmas, 68.
Noȝt, nought, 680, 694, 961.
Nurne. See *Norne*.
Nurned, proffered, 1771.
Nurture, 919, 1661.
Nwe, new, anew, 60, 636, 1668.
Nweȝ, news, tidings, 1407.
Nw-ȝer,) New-year, 60, 105,
Nwe-ȝer,) 284.
Nw-ȝeres,) New-year's, 454,
Nwe-ȝereȝ,) 1054, 1669.
*Nye,) difficulty, trouble, harm,
Nyȝe,) 58, 2002, 2141.

Nye, to harm, assault, 1575.
Nykked with nay, denied, 706.
*Nyme, to take, 993, 2141.
Nys, nice, strange, 323, 358.
Nysen (*pres. pl.*), become foolish, 1266.

O, of, 615.
Of, from, 183, 519, 1413; off, 773, 1332, 1607.
Of-kest, cast off, 1147.
Oghe, ought, 1526.
Olde, 1440. See *For-olde.*
On, one, 30, 206, 864, 952; in, 867, 969.
On-chasyng=a-chasing, a-hunting, 1143.
On-coolde, sorrowfully, 2474.
*On-dryʒe=on-dreʒe=adreʒ, aside, 1031.
One, alone, unaccompanied, 2118; *hym one,* 904; *oure one,* 1230, 2245.
Onewe, anew, 65.
Oneʒ, once, 1090.
On-ferum, afar, 1575.
On fyrst, at first, 301, 491, 1477.
On-huntyng, a hunting, 1102.
On-hyʒt, on high, aloft, above, 421.
On-lenthe, afar, 232, 1231.
On-life,) alive, in life, 385, 1717,
On-lyue,) 1786.
On-lofte, aloft, above, 788, 2261.
On-loghe, below, down, 1373.
On-nyʒtes, at night, in the night, 47, 693.
On (vp)-slepe, asleep, 244.
On-stray, astray, aside, 1716.
Onsware, to answer, 275.
Onswareʒ, answers, 386.
Or, than, 1543.
Oritore, oratory, 2190.
*Orpedly, boldly, 2232.
Oryʒt, aright, 40.
Ostel, mansion, 253. See *Hostel.*
Other, or, 9, 702, 1246; either, 2216.

Other-whyle, other times, 722.
Oute, throughout, wholly, 1511.
Outtrage, surprising, 29.
Oueral, everywhere, 630.
Ouer-thwert, athwart, across, 1438.
Ouer-walt, overcome, overturned, 314. See *Walt.*
Ouer-ʒede, passed over, 500.
Oʒt, ought, 300, 1815.
*Oʒt=aʒt, bold, 2215.

Pane, cloth, 154. O.Fr. *pane.*
Paneʒ (*pl.*), 855.
*Papiayeʒ, parrots, 611.
Papure, paper, 802.
Paraunter, peradventure, 2343.
Pared, cut, 802.
Park, 769.
Passande, passing, 1014.
Patrounes, sovereigns, 6.
Paumeʒ, antlers, 1155.
Paunce, coat of mail, 2017.
*Payeʒ, pleases, 1379.
Payne, to be at pains, endeavour, 1042.
*Payre, to injure, impair, 1734.
Payred, failed, 650, 1456.
Payttrure, defence for the neck of a horse, 168, 601.
Pelure, costly fur, 154.
Pelures (*pl.*), furs, 2029.
Pendauntes,) the dropping orna-
Pendaunteʒ,) ments of horse-
trappings or a girdle, 168, 2038, 2431.
Penyes, pence, money, 79.
Pentangel,) figure of five points,
Pentaungel,) 620, 636, 664.
Pented, pertained, 204.
Pernyng, picking and dressing, a term applied to birds, 611.
*Pertly, openly, promptly, 544, 1941.
Pes, peace, 266.
Pese=pays, measure, weight, 2364. See Gloss. to Hampole.
Peter! an oath used as Mary! 813.

Piched, } fastened, 576 : situated,
Pyched, } fixed, 768.
*Piked, } ornamented, cleaned,
Pyked, } burnished, 769, 2017.
Pyned, enclosed, fortified (?), 769.
(Perhaps a mistake for *pynacled*.
Sir F. Madden).
Pypyng, 1017.
*Pine, } trouble, grief, pain, tor-
Pyne, } ment, 123, 747, 1812,
1985.
Piped, 747.
Pitosly, 747.
Piȝt. See *Pyȝt*.
Plate, 583.
Plateȝ, steel armour for the body,
2017.
Plesaunce, pleasure, 1247.
Plesaunt, 808.
Plytes, straits, 733.
Plyȝt; harm, danger, 266 ; offence,
fault, 2393.
Polaynes, knee-pieces in a suit of
armour, 576. This term for
genouillieres is found in the
household book of Edward the
First.
Policed, } polished, 576, 2038 ;
Polysed, } made clean, absolved,
Polyst, } 2393.
Porter, 808.
Poudred, 800.
Pouer, poor, 768.
Poynt, condition, 2049 ; to declare,
write, 1009.
Praunce, 2064.
Prayere, meadow, 768. Fr. *prairie*.
Prayse, estimate, appraise, 1850.
Prece, proceed, 2097.
Presed, thronged, 830.
*Prestly, promptly, 757, 911.
Preué, privy, secret, 902.
Preue, to prove, 262.
Preued, proved, 79.
Prik, to gallop, 2049.
Pryme, *prime*, six o'clock in the
morning, 1175.

Pris, } price, worth, estimation,
Prys, } excellence, 1247; 1277,
1770, 1850, 2364; reward, prize,
1379, 1630.
Prise, fine, good, 1945.
Prowes, prowess, valour, courage,
912, 1249.
Prys, note of the horn in hunting,
after breaking up the game,
1362, 1601.
Pure, quite, perfect, 808, 1247.
Pured, refined, pure, 633, 912,
1737, 2393.
Pured, furred, 154.
Pynakle, 800.
Pyne, to take pains, 1538.
Pyned, 1009.
Pysan, gorget of mail or plate at-
tached to the helmet, 204.
Pyth, strength, power, 1456.
Pyȝt, pitched, fixed, 1456, 1734.

Quat, what, 233, 460.
Quat, how ! lo ! 563, 2201.
Quat-so, whatsoever, 255.
Quaynt, 999.
Quel, while, 822.
Queldepoyntes, hassocks (?), 877.
*Quelle, to put an end to, 752 ;
kill, 1449, 2109.
Quelled, slain, 1324.
*Queme, good, pleasant, 578, 2109.
Quen, } when, 20, 130, 497.
Quhen, }
Quere, where, 1058.
Quer-fore, wherefore, 1294.
Quere-so, wheresoever, 644, 1227,
1490.
Querré, quarry. 1324. Fr. *curée*.
To *make the quarry* = to break
up the deer, and feed the hounds
on the skin
Quest, united cry of the hounds,
1150, 1421.
Quethe, cry, clamour, 1150. A.S.
cwéthan, to call ; *cwithe*, a saying.
Quethen = whethen = whence, 461.

Redly, } readily, 373, 392.
Redily, }

Refourme, renew, remake, 378.

*Rehayted, cheered, encouraged, 895, 1422, 1744.

Reherce, 1213.

Rehersed, 392.

*Rekenly,nobly,worthily,princely, 39, 251, 821.

*Rele, to encounter, 2246.

*Reled, swaggered, 229 ; rolled, spread, 304.

Remene, to remember, 2483.

Remorde, to blame, 2434.

*Remwe, to remove, change, 1475.

*Renay, refuse, 1827.

*Renayed, refused, 1821.

*Renk, } man, knight, 303, 691,
Renke, }   1558, 1821.

Renkkes, } men, 432, 862, 1134,
Renkke₃, }   2246.

Rennande, running, 857.

*Renne, to run, 1568.

Rennes, } runs, 310, 731, 1570.
Renne₃, }

Repayre, 1016.

Require, 1056.

*Res, swift course, pace, 1164, 1899.

Resayt, a hunting term applied to the stations taken up by those on foot, 1168.

Rescowe, rescue, 2308.

*Resette, place of reception, abode, 2164.

Respite, 297.

Restayed, stopt, driven back, 1153.

Resteyed, constrained, 1672.

Reue, to take away, bereave, 2459.

Reuel, 311, 538.

Reuerence, 251, 1243.

Rewarde, 1610.

Richchande, running, 1898.

Richen, dress, 1130.

*Ricchis, } goes, 8 ; prepares,
Riches, } dresses, 1309, 1873.
Ryches, }

Riche, } noble, proud, powerful,
Ryche, }   8, 20, ·39, 40, 397, 1744. Used substantively in the plural, *nobles*, 66, 362.

Riche, *sb.* horse (?), 2177.

Richley, } proudly, nobly, 308,
Rychely, }   931.

Rimed, spoke loudly, 308. A.S. *hreman*.

Roche, rock, 2199.

Rocher, rock 1432.

Rocheres, } rocks, 1327, 1698.
Rochere₃, }

Rode, rood, 1949.

Rof, blow, cut, 2346 ; evidently from O.E. *rive*, to tear, cut.

Rogh, }
Roghe, } rough,•shaggy, 745,1432,
Ro₃, }   1608,1898,2162,2198.
Ro₃e, }

Rokked, rolled, knocked off, cleansed, 2018.

" Geoffrey of Vinesauf says, ' *Rotantur loricæ, ne rubigine squalescunt,*' which, Sir S. Meyrick adds, was done by putting the coat of mail into a barrel filled with sand and rolling it about."
(Crit. Inq , l. 85.)

Rome₃ =roams, walks, proceeds, 2198.

Rone₃, thickets, brushwood, 1466.

"Thane thay reode by that ryuer, that rynnyd so swythe,
Thare the ryndez overrechez with realle bowghez ;
The roo and the rayne-dere reklesse thare rovene
In *ranez* and in rosers to ryotte thame-selvene."
(Morte Arthure, p. 78.)

Ronge (*pret.* of *ringe*), resounded, clattered, 2204.

"Hys armour *ryngis* or *clattirs* horribly."
(G. Douglas, vol. ii., p. 576.)

Ronk, beautiful, 513.

Ronkkled, wrinkled, 953.

Rote, in phrase *bi-rote* = cheerfully, confidently, 2207. A.S. *rót*,

cheerful. Cf. *root-fast*, firm,
steadfast (A.S. *rót-fæst*). This
term is left unexplained by Sir
F. Madden.
*Roun, to whisper, commune, 362,
Rounce, steed, 303. O.E. *runci*.
Fr. *roncin*.
*Rous,=rose, praise, fame, 310.
Roust, rust, 2018.
Route, violent movement, impetus,
457.
Roue, cleaved, cut, 2346; *pret.* of
rive.
Roueʒ, roofs, 799.
Roʒ,
Roʒe, } rough. See *Rogh*.
*Ruchched,) ordered, fixed, set-
Ruched, } tled, 303,367, 2219.
See *Riches*.
*Rudede, streaked with red, ruddy,
1695. Cf. O.E. *rode* and *ruddon*.
Rudeleʒ, curtains, canopies, 857.
Ruful, 2076.
Rugh,) rough, 953, 2166. See
Ruʒe, } *Rogh*.
*Runisch, violent, impetuous, 457.
*Runischly, fiercely, roughly, 304.
Runyschly, violently, 432.
*Rurd,) noise, clamour, 1149,
Rurde, } 1698, 1916.
*Ruthes, moves, dresses, 1558.
Ryalme, realm, 310, 691.
*Rych, direct, 1223. See *Riches*.
Ryches, goes, prepares. See *Riches*.
Ryched, enriched, 599.; prepared,
2206.
Ryd,) =rid, to release, 364;
Rydde, } separate, 2246. A.S.
riddan.
Ryde, proceed, 1344.
Rygge, back, 1344, 1608.
Rymeʒ, skirts, 1343. A.S. *reama*.
O.E. *reme*, membrane, rim. See
Rym in Glossary to Hampole.
*Ryngeʒ =rynkeʒ =renkeʒ = men,
2018.
Rynk, ring, 1817, 1827.

Ryol, royal, 2036.
Rypeʒ, become ripe, 528.
Rys, bough, twig, 1698. A.S. *hris*.
*Rytte=ryte, cut, rip, 1332. Fris.
ryte.
*Ryue=ryfe=rife, much, 2046.
Ryueʒ, rips, rives, cuts, 1341, 2290.
Ryʒt, addressed, prepared, 308.

Sabatounʒ, steel shoes, 574. Fr.
sabot. Spanish *sapato*.
Sadel, *sb.* 437; *vb.* 1128.
Sadly, gravely, steadily, 437, 1593,
1937, 2409.
Saf, save, except, 394.
Sage=segge=man, 531.
*Sale, hall, 197, 243, 349.
Salue, to salute, 1473.
Salure, salt-cellar, 886.
*Same,) together, 50, 363, 673,
Samen, } 744, 1318.
*Samen, to assemble, 1372.
Samned, joined, 659.
Sauer, safer, 1202.
Saverly, savourly, carefully, 1937,
2048.
Saw,) saying, speech, 1202, 1246.
Saʒe, }
Saʒeʒ, words, 341.
Saylande, flowing, 865.
Sayn, girdle, 589.
*Sayned, blessed, 761, 1202.
Saynt, rich stuff, Fr. *samit*, 2431.
Scade=schade, divided, severed,
425.
*Scathe, harm, 674, 2353.
Schadden, shed, dropt, 727.
Schafte, spear, 205.
Schafted, set, sank, 1467.
Schale, shall, 1240.
*Schalk, man, knight, 160, 424,
562, 1776, 2061, 2372.
Schalkeʒ, men, knights, 1454.
Seham, 317.
Schamed, 1189.
Schankes, legs, 160.
Schap, was formed, shapen, 2328.

8

Schape, direct (?), 1210. Sir F. Madden suggests *escape*.
Schapen, shaped, 213.
Schapes, relates, 1626.
Scharp, used substantively for sword, 1593, 1902; axe, 2318.
Schaterande, dashing, 2083.
Schawe, to show, 27.
*Schaʒe, grove, wood, 2161.
Scheder=schedes(?),drifts(?),956.
Schedeʒ, pours, 506.
Scheldeʒ, shields of a bear, 1456, 1626.
*Schemered=shimered, glittered, 772.
*Schend, } to destroy, confound,
Schende, } 2266.
*Schene, bright, beautiful, 662, 2314; used substantively, 2268.
Schere=chere, countenance, mien, 334.
Scher, cut, 1337.
Schere, to cut, shear, 213.
Scho, she, 1259, 1550, 1555.
Scholes, hangs down (?), 160.
Schonkes, } legs, 431, 846.
Schonkeʒ, }
Schore, shore, earth, 2161, 2332.
Schoreʒ (*pl.*), 2083.
Schotten, shot, 1167.
Schowued, shoved, fell with force, 2083.
Schowen (*pl. pres.*), shove, push, 1454.
Schowueʒ, shoves, pushes, 2161.
Schrank, sunk, pierced, 425, 2313.
Schrof, shrived, 1880.
Schunt, a shunt, flinching, 2268.
Schunt, shunted, flinched, shrunk, 1902, 2280.
Schwne=shun, protect,defend,205.
Schylde, forbid, 1776.
*Schyn, shall, 2401.
*Schyr, } fair, bright, clear, 317,
Schyre, } 425, 619, 772; used
Schyire, } substantively for *skin*, neck, 2256.

Schyre, fairly, clearly, 506, 2083.
Schyrer, fairer, clearer, 955.
Schyrly, cleanly, 1880.
Scowtes, high rocks (?), 2167.
Sech, seek, 1052.
Seche, such, 1543.
Sege, } siege, 1, 2525.
Segge, }
*Segg, } man, knight, 96, 115, 226,
Segge, } 394, 437, 574.
Segges, } men, 673, 822, 1438.
Seggeʒ, }
Seghe, saw, 1705.
*Seker=siker, sure, trusty, faithful, 265, 403.
Selden, seldom, 499.
*Sele, good fortune, prosperity, 1938, 2409, 2422.
Sellokest, most surprising, 1439.
*Selly, marvel, wonder, 475, 2170.
Selly, strange, 28; wondrously, 1194.
Sellyeʒ, wonders, 239.
Sellyly, strangely, wondrously, 963, 1803.
Sellyly=selly, excellent, 1962.
Selure, canopy, 76.
Seluen, self, 51, 107, 113, 1548.
Semblaunce,}countenance, appear-
Semblaunt, } ance, behaviour, 148, 468, 1273, 1658.
Semble, assembly, 1429.
*Seme, seemly, proper, 1085.
Semed, beseemed, befitted,73,1929.
Semely, comely, fair, 672, 685.
Semeʒ, seams, borders, 610.
Semly, } fairly, suitably, becom-
Semlych, } ingly, courteously, 865, 882, 916, 1198, 1658.
Semloker, more seemly, fairer, 83.
Semlyly, becomingly, 622.
Sendal, fine silk, 76. According to Ducange it is a species of camelot.
Sene, truthful (?), 148, 341. O.Sw. *sann*, true.
Sene, to see, 712.

*Sere, several, 124, 632, 761, 822, 1982; diverse, 889, 2417; separately, 1522.
*Serlepes, severally, by turns, 301.
Sertayn, certainly, 174.
Serued, deserved, 1380.
Seruyce, 751.
Sese, to receive, 1825.
Sesed, held, seized, 822, 1330.
Sesed, ceased, 1, 1083, 2526.
Sete = swete (?), 889.
Settel, seat, chair, 882.
Seuer, to part, 1983.
Seueres, parts, 1797.
*Sewe, prepared dish of meat, perhaps a stew, 892.
Sewes (pl.), 124, 889.
Seye, to go, 1879.
Seȝ, Seȝe, Seȝen, } saw, 672, 707, 1619, 1911.
Seȝen, arrived, 1958.
Sidbordeȝ, 115.
*Siker, } sure, trusty, brave, 96,
Syker, } 115, 2048, 2493.
Siker, surely, 163.
Siker, vb. to pledge, "siker my trawthe" = pledge my word (troth), 1673; assure, 394.
Sille, seat, 55. A.S. sylla, a chair.
Skayued, wild, 2167. See note, p. 83.
Skere = shere = pure, modest, 1261. A.S. scir.
Skete, quickly, 19.
*Skweȝ, clouds (?), shadows (?), 2167. Sir F. Madden suggests groves, shady coverts.
*Skyfted = shifted, changed, 19.
*Skyl, } reason, 1296, 1509.
Skylle, }
Skynneȝ, in phrase any skynneȝ = anys-kynneȝ = any kind of, 1539.
Skyrteȝ, horse-trappings, 601; skirts of a robe, 865.
*Slade, valley, 2147.
Slades, vallies, 1159.

Slaked, ceased, 244. See note, p. 81.
Slentyng, shooting, glancing, 1160. See note, p. 82.
Slete, 729.
*Sleȝe, ingenious, 797, 893.
Sleȝly, slyly, softly, 1182.
*Sleȝt, } stratagem, 1854, 1858.
Sliȝt, }
Sleȝteȝ = sleights, contrivances, 916.
Slode = slided, slipt, 1182.
Sloke (vb. imp.), stop, cease (talking), 412. O.N. sloka. See note, p. 81.
Slomeryng, slumbering, 1182.
Slot, pit of the stomach, 1330, 1593. According to some slot is the hollow above the breast-bone.
"O-slante-doune fro the slote he slyttes at ones."
(Morte Arthure, p. 189.)
Slypped, fallen, 244.
Slyȝt, skilful, 1542.
Smartly, quickly, 407.
Smeten, smote, 1763.
Smethely, smoothly, 1789.
*Smolt, mild, 1763.
Smothely, perfectly, 407.
Snart, severely, sharply, 2003. O.N. snart.
Snawe, snow, 956.
Snayped, nipped, 2003. O.E. snaip, to snub, nip, pierce. O.N. sneipa.
Snitered, drove, drifted, 2003.
Soiourned, lodged, 2048.
Solace, 570.
Sop, hasty meal, 1135.
Sore, grieved, 1826, 1983.
*Sorȝe, imprecation, 1721; sorrow, 2415.
Sostnaunce, 1095.
*Soth, } truth, 84, 355.
Sothe, }
Sothen, boiled, sodden, 892.
Sothly, truly, 673, 978.
Sounde (in-sounde, well, unhurt, 2489.

Sounder, herd of wild swine, 1440.
Soundyly, soundly, 1991.
*Sourquydrye, pride, 311.
*Sowme, number, 1321.
Soʒt, went, departed, 685, 1488.
Spare-wise, moderately, temperately, 901.
Sparlyr, calf of the leg, 158. See Wyclif, Deuteron, xxviii., 35.
Sparthe, battle axe, 209.
Sped, hastened, went quickly, 1444.
Spede, profit, 918.
Speded, hastened, 979.
Spedeʒ, prosperest, 410.
Spedly, expediently, 1935.
Spek,   ⎫
Speken, ⎬ spake, 1117, 1288.
*Spelle, speech, narrative, 209, 1199, 2184.
Spelleʒ, talkest, 2140.
Spend,   ⎫ fastened, 158, 587. O.N.
Spenet, ⎭ spenna.
Spende (speche), to talk, 410.
Spenne, space, interval, 1074, 2316.
Spenné, spinny, quickset hedge, 1709, 1896.
Spetos, sharp, cruel, 209.
Sponeʒ, spoons, 886.
Sporeʒ, spurs, 587.
Sprenged, sprang, 1415; dawned, 2009.
Sprent, leapt, 1896.
Sprit, started, 2316.
Sprong, sprang, 670.
*Spured, ⎫ =spered, inquired, 901,
Spuryed, ⎭   2093.
Spyt, injury, 1444.
Stabled, established, 1069.
Stablye, station of huntsmen, 1153.
*Stad, placed, disposed, 33, 644, 2137.
Staf-ful, quite full, 494.
*Stale, ⎫ seat, 104, 107.
Stalle, ⎭
Stalked, approached, moved, 237.
*Stalworth, strong, powerful, brave, 846, 1659.

Stange, pole, staff, 1614. A.S. stenge. S.Prov.E. stang.
Stapled, furnished with staples, 981.
*Starande, glittering, 1818.
Start, started, moved, 431, 1716.
Statut, agreement, covenant, 1060.
Staue, staff, 2139.
*Sted,   ⎫ place, 439, 2213, 2323.
Stedde, ⎭
*Stek, stuck, 152.
*Stel, stole, 1191.
Stel-gere, steel-gear, armour, 260.
*Stemed,   ⎫ stood still, stopt, 230,
Stemmed, ⎭   1117.
*Steuen, voice, sound, 242, 2008, 2336; conference, 1060, 2194, 2213.
Stif, strong, brave, 104, 107, 322.
Stif, courageously, 671.
Stifly, 287, 605.
Stirop, 2060.
Stithly, ⎫ stiffly, strongly, 431,
Stythly, ⎭   575. A.S. stith, strong.
*Stiʒtel, to dispose, 2137.
Stiʒtles, ⎫ sits, dwells, 104, 2213.
Stiʒtleʒ, ⎭
Stoffed, 606.
*Stoken (p.p. of steke), secured, fastened, fixed, 33, 494, 782, 2194.
Ston-stil, 242.
Stonyed, confounded, astonished, 1291.
Stor,   ⎫ strong, great, 1291, 1923.
Store, ⎭ A.S. stór, great, vast.
Stori, 34.
Stoundeʒ, time, 1567; bi-stoundeʒ, at times, 1517.
Stowned, confounded, astonished, 242, 301.
Strakande, blowing, 1364, 1923. A hunting term.
Strayne, restrain, curb, 176.
Streʒt, close, tight, 152.
Strok, stroke, 287.
Stroked (beard), 334.

Strokes, brandishes, 416.
*Strothe, rugged, wild, 1710. See note, p. 83.
Strye, destroy, 2194.
Strythe,) position of the legs
Stryththe,) when firmly placed, stride, 846, 2305.
Stubbe, stook of a tree, 2293.
Sture₃=stirs, brandishes, 331.
Sturne, stout, bold, 143; used substantively, 214.
Sturnely, 381.
Sturtes, stirrups, 171.
Stylly, softly, 1117.
Sty₃tel, set, dispose, 2252.
Suande, following, 1467.
Sued, followed, 501, 1705.
Sues, follows, 510.
Sumned, summoned, 1052.
Sum-quat, somewhat, 86.
Sum-quyle,) once, formerly, 625,
Sum-whyle,) 720.
Sundred, severed, disjointed, 659.
Sure, 588.
Surfet, fault, 2433.
Surquidre, pride, 2457.
Swange, loins, 138, 2034. O.Sw. swange.
Swap, exchange, 1108.
*Sware, square, 138.
*Sware, answer, 1108.
Swared, answered, 1793, 2011.
Sware₃, answers, 1756.
*Swenged, rushed, 1439.
Swengen, proceed, move quickly, 1615.
Swenges, starts, rushes, 1756.
Swere, swear, 403; swore, 1825.
*Swete, "in swete"= in life, 2518. Sir F. Madden renders it suit.
Swete, adj. used substantively, 1108, 1222.
Swete=sweet, fine, good, 180. Sir F. Madden renders it sweated.
Swethled, folded, 2034. A.S. swethel, a swaddling-band.
*Sweuenes, dreams, 1756.

*Sweyed, moved, pressed, 1429.
*Swe₃,) follows, 1562; stooped,
Swe₃e) 1796.
Swyere₃, squires, 824.
*Swynge₃, rushes, 1562. See Swenge₃.
*Swyre, neck, throat, 138,186,957.
*Swythe, quickly, 8, 815, 1424, 2259; greatly, earnestly, 1860, 1866, 1897.
Swythely, quickly, much, 1479.
Swoghe (silence), dead (silence), 243. A.S. swugian, to be silent. mute, astonished.
*Syfle₃, blows, whistles, 517.
Sykande, sighing, 1796.
*Syked, sighed, 672.
*Syker, sure. See Siker.
Sykyng, sighing, 753.
Syluener=sylueren, adj. used substantively, silver, plate, 124.
Syluer-in, silver, 886.
Symple, 503.
Syngne, sign, token, 625.
*Syn, since, 19, 24, 919, 1892.
*Sythe,) times, 17, 632, 761,
Sythes,) 1868.
Sythe₃,)
Sythen, since, afterwards, next, 1, 6, 43, 115, 358, 1234, 1339.
Sy₃,) saw, 83, 200, 1582.
Sy₃e,)

Ta, take, 413, 2357.
Table₃, corbels (?), 789.
Tachched,) attached, fixed, 219,
Tached,) 2512.
Tache₃, fastens, 2176.
*Takles, gear, 1129.
Tale, speech, discourse, 1236.
Talenttyf, desirous, 350.
Talkande, talking, 108.
Talkyng, speech, 917.
Tan (pl.), take, 977, 1920.
Tan, taken, 490, 1210.
Tape,) stroke, blow, 406, 2357.
Tappe,)

Tapit, carpet, 568; table (?), 884.

Tapites, } tapestry, 77, 858.
Tapyteȝ, }

Tars is stated by Ducange to mean *Tharsia*, a country adjoining to Cathay, but not to be confounded with Tartary. In 77, 858, it is named as the place where tapestries were manufactured, and in 571 a rich silk must be understood.

Taysed=teased (?), driven, harassed, 1169.

*Tayt, lively, sportive, 988, and hence active, fierce, 1377. Sir F. Madden suggests *fair, plump*.

"The bustuns bukkis rakis furth on raw, Heyrdis of hertis throw the thyk wodschaw, Kyddis skippand throw ronnys efter rays, In lyssouris and on leys; litill lammys Full *tayt* and tryg socht bletand to thar dammys."

(G. Douglas, vol. ii., p. 758.)

Taȝt, } taught, 1485, 2379.
Taȝtte, }

*Teccheles, blameless, 917.

*Tech, disposition, quality, 2488.

Teches (*pl.* of *tech*), 2436.

*Telde, mansion, habitation, 11, 1775.

Telded, set up, built, 795, 884.

Teldet, set up, 1648.

Teldes, habitations, 11.

Temes, stories, themes, 1541.

*Tene, *sb.* sorrow, mischief, 22.

Tene, *adj.* tedious, perilous, difficult, 1008, 1707, 2075.

Tene, *vb.* to grieve, 2002.

Tened, grieved, 2501; molested, 1169.

Teneȝ, troubles, matters, 547.

Tenelyng, trouble (?), 1514.

*Tent, *sb.* care, intent, attention, 624.

Tented, took care of, 1018.

Thar, need, 2354. A.S. *thearfan.*

That, used for *what*, 1406.

Thaȝ, though, 350, 438, 467.

*Thede, country, land, 1499.

Theder, thither, 935.

Then, than, 24, 236, 655.

Ther, } where, 353, 428, 874.
There, }

Ther-forne, therefore, 1107.

Ther-tylle, thereto, 1110, 1369.

*Thewes, } manners, 912, 916.
Thewcȝ, }

Thinkkeȝ, } seems, 1111, 1241,
Thynkkeȝ, } 1481, 1793, 2109.

*Tho, those, 68, 466; the, 39, 1419.

Thof, though, 624.

*Tholed, suffered, 1859, 2419.

Thonk, thanks, 1380.

Thonke, thank, 1984.

Thonkkeȝ, thanks, 1031.

Thore, there, 667.

Thoȝt, seemed, 49, 803, 819, 870.

Thrast, thrust, 1443.

*Thrat, threatened, 1713; compelled, urged, 1980.

Thrawen, bound, twisted, 194. A.S. *thrdwan*, to wind.

*Thrawen, brawny, 579. In G. Douglas *thrawin* has the sense of fierce, bold, strong.

Thred, 1712.

*Threpe, chiding, 1859, 2997.

Threpeȝ, chides, reproves, and hence struggles with, 504.

Threted, threatened, 1725.

*Thrich, push, rush, 1713.

*Thro, earnest, eager, 645, 1713, 1751, 1868, 1946; quickly, 1021; bold, confident, 2300.

*Throly, earnestly, 939.

*Thronge, thrust, crowded, 1021.

Throw, time, while, 1680, 2219. A.S. *thrah.*

Throwen=thrown=exposed, 1740. Sir F. Madden takes it to be another form of *thrawen*, plump.

Thrye, thrice, 763.

Thryes, thrice, 1936.

*Thrynge₃, crowdest, 2397.

*Thrynne, three, 1868.

Thryuande, hearty, 1980.

Thryuandely, heartily, 1080, 1380.

*Thryuen, well favoured, 1740.

*Thry₃t, threw, 1443; given, 1946.

Thulged=tholged=tholed, endured, 1859. A.S. *tholgian*, to endure, suffer.

*Thurled=thirled, pierced, 1356.

Thur₃, } through, above, 91, 243,
Thur₃e, } 645.

Thu₃t, thought, 843, 848.

Thwarle, tight, hard, 194. *Wharlknot* is still used in the same sense in Lancashire.

Thwong, thong, 194.

Thwonges, thongs, 579.

Thy, therefore (?), 2247.

Thy₃e₃, thighs, 579.

*Tit, }
Tyt, } quickly, steadily, promptly,
Tite, } 31, 299, 1596. See
Tyte, } *As-tyt.*

Titleres, hounds, 1726.

To, too, 1827.

To=te, go, 1671.

To-fylched, seized, pulled down, 1172.

To-hewe, to cut in pieces, 1853.

*Tole, weapon, axe, 413, 2260.

*Tolke, man, 1775, 1811, 1966. See *Tulk.*

To-morn, } to-morrow, 548, 756,
To-morne, } 1097.

Tone=tane, betaken, committed, 2159.

Toppyng, mane (?), or top, head (?), 191.

Tor, tedious, difficult, 165, 719. O.N. *tor* (a prefixal element denoting difficulty, trouble, etc.)

To-raced, run down, 1168.

Torche, 1119.

Toret=turreted, 960.

Tornayee₃, turns, wheels, 1707.

Tortors, turtles, 612.

Toruayle=labour, task, 1540. O.N. *torvelldr.* O. Scotch, *torfel,* to be fatigued, to pine away.

To-tachched, fastened, tied, 579.

Totes, peeps, looks, 1476. Swed. *titta.*

Tournayed, 41.

*Towch, request, 1301.

Towches, sounds, 120.

Towche₃, covenants, 1677.

Towen, come, drawn, 1093. A.S. *teón* (*p.p. togen, ge-togen*), to pull, draw, to go.

To₃t, *adj.* behaved, mannered, 1869. Northumbrian *ta₃t.* O.E. *tau₃t.*

Trammes, stratagems, 3.

Trantes, employs artifices or tricks, 1707. See Townely Mysteries, v. *Trant.*

Trased, twiped, 1739.

Tranayl, fatigue, labour, 2241.

Trauayled, travelled, 1093.

Traunt, trick, 1700. See *Trantes.*

Trauthe, } troth, faith, fidelity,
Traweth, } 403, 626, 1050,
Trawthe, } 1545, 1638.

Trawe, to believe, 70, 90, 1396; *imp.* trust, 2112.

Trayle₃, hunt by the track or scent, 1700.

Trayst, assured, 1211.

Trayteres=trayueres=trauerce (?), 1700.

Treleted, adorned, 960.

Tressoun, head-dress, 1739.

Trestes, } trestles, supports of a
Treste₃, } table, 884, 1648.

Tricherie, treachery, 4.

Tried, 4.

Trifel, } 108, 547.
Trifle, }

*Trochet, a term of architecture, 795.

*Trowe, to believe, 813, 2238.

True, *adj.* used substantively= truth (?), 1210.

Trulofe;, true-love knots, 612.

Trumpes, } trumpets, 116, 1016.
Trumpe;, }

*Trussen, pack up, 1129.

Trwe, true, 1091, 1514, 1845.

Trwluf, } true-love, 1527, 1540.
Trweluf, }

Tryed, fine, costly, good, 77, 219.

Tryst, trust, 380.

Tryster, } The stations alloted
Trysteres, } to different persons
in hunting, 1146, 1170, 1712.

Trystyly, faithfully, 2348.

Tule=tuly (?), 568.

*Tulk, man, knight, 3, 638, 2133.

*Tulkes, men, 41.

Tuly seems to be equivalent, 858, to Toulouse, 77, which place seems then to have been famed for its tapestries.

Tusche;, tusks, 1563, 1579.

Tweyne, two, twain, 962, 1339.

Twyes, twice, 1522.

*Twynne, to sever, part, 2512.

Twynne, two, 425.

Twynnen, twined, 191.

Tyffen, to array, put in order, 1129. O.N. typpa.

Tylle, to, 673, 1979.

*Tyrnen, flayed, 1921.

*Tyt, promptly, speedily, 1596.

Tytelet, commencement, chief, 1515.

Tyxt, text, 1515, 1541.

*Ty;t, fastened, tied, 568, 858.

Ty;t, undertake or endeavour (?), 2483.

*Vch, } each, 101, 131, 628, 995,
Vche, }

Vcha=Northumbrian ilka, each, 742, 997, 1262.

Vchon, } each one, 98, 657,
Vchone, } 1113.

*Vgly, horrible, 441; horribly, 2079.

*Vmbe, around, about, 589, 1830, 2034.

Vmbe-clypped, encircled, embraced, 616.

Vmbe-foldes, encircles, falls about, 181.

Vmbe-kesten, surrounded, 1434.

Vmbe-lappe;, enfolds, 628.

Vmbe-te;e, inclosed, 770; te;e is from the A.S. teogan, to draw, teah, drew.

Vmbe-torne (=about, around (?), Sir F. M.)=about-turned (?)= twisted (?).

Vmbe-weued, enclosed, 581.

Vnbarred, 2070.

Vn-bene, rugged, impassable, 710. See Bene.

Vnblythe, mournful, sorrowful, sad, 746.

Vncely, mischievous, 1562.

Vncouth, strange, marvellous, 93, 1808.

Vndo, to cut up game; a hunting term, 1327.

*Vnethe, scarcely, 134.

*Vnhap, misfortune, 438, 2511.

Vnhardeled, dispersed, 1697. Fr. hardelle, troupe.

Vnlace, to cut up, 1606.

Vnleute, disloyalty, 2499.

Vn-louked, unlocked, 1201.

Vn-mete, immense, 208.

Vn-rydely, ruggedly, 1432. O.E. unryde, sharp, rough. A.S. ungerydu, rugged; ungerydelice, sharply; geryd, smooth, even.

Vn-slayn, not slain, 1858.

Vn-sly;e, careless.

Vn-soundyly, fiercely, 1438.

Vn-sparely, unsparingly, 979.

Vn-spurd, unasked, 918. See Spured.

Vn-thryuande, uncourteous, 1499.

Vn-trawthe, unfaithfulness, 2383, 2509.

Vn-ty;tel, if not an error for vntyl ny;te, may mean unrestrainedly (from ty;t, to fasten). Sir F.

Madden renders it merrily. See *Ty3t.*

Vp-brayde, drawn up, 781.

Vpon, at, 9, 301, 1934.

Vrysoun, the same as the *cointesse* or "kerchef of plesaunce," 608. Fr. *hourson.*

Vtter, out, outward, 1565.

Vayles, veils, 958.

Vayres, purity, 1015. Left unexplained by Sir F. Madden.

Ver, man, knight, 866. O.N. *ver.*

Verayly, 866.

Verdure, green, 161.

Vertuus=vertuous, precious, 2027.

Vewters, men who tracked deer by the *fewte* or odour, 1146.

Visage, 866.

Voyde, to quit, 346.

Voyded, got rid of, 1518; void, free, 634.

Voyde3, casts, 1342.

Vyage, expedition, journey, 535.

Vylany, ⎫ fault, 345, 634.
Vylanye, ⎭

Wage, surety (?), 533.

Wages, 396.

Waked, kept awake, sat up at night, 1094.

*Wakkest, weakest, 354.

*Wakned, awakened, 119; shone, 1650.

*Wale, to seek, 398; choose or possess, 1238.

*Wale, lovely, worthy, 1010; choice, good, 1712, 1759.

Waled, chosen, 1276.

Walke3, spreads, 1521.

Walle=wale, excellent, 1403.

*Wallande, boiling, ferment, 1762.

*Walt, threw, cast, 1336. O.N. *vellta.*

*Walt, exercised, possessed, 231; enjoyed, 485.

*Waltered, poured, was shed, 684.

*Wan, came, 2231.

Wande, bough, branch, 1161.

*Wane, wanting, deficient, 493.

*Wap, blow, 2249.

*Wapped, flew with violence, as an arrow; rushed as the wind, 2004. O.N. *vappa.*

War! exclamation of the hunters, 1158.

"In the *Maister of the Game,* in the instructions for hunting the hare, the horsemen are directed 'for to kepe that none hownde folowe to sheepe, ne to other beestis, and if thei do, to ascrie hem sore, and bilaisshe hem wel, saying lowde, *Ware! Ware! ha, ha! Ware!'* "—MS. Cott., Vesp. B. xii., fol. 97*b.*

War, aware, 764, 1586.

Ware, to use, employ, 402, 1235.

Waret, acted, dealt, 2344.

Warly, warily, 1186, 1900.

Warloker, more warily, 677.

*Warp, cast, 2253; cast, uttered, 224, 1423, 2025.

*Warthe, water-ford, 715.

Waryst, protected, 1094.

Wast, waist, 144.

Waste, wilderness, 2098.

*Wathe=wothe, injury, danger, 2355.

Wat3, was, *passim.* had, 1413.

Waunden, wound, bound, 215.

*Wayke, weak, 282.

*Wayned, brought, 264, 984, 1032, 2456; sent, 2459.

*Wayne3 (=wayue3?), raises, 1743.

*Wayte, to see, 306.

Wayted, looked, 2163.

Wayte3, watches, looks, 1186, 2289.

Wayth, game, venison, 1381.

Wayued, stroked, moved, 306.

We! ah! 2185.

*Wede, armour, clothing, part of the dress, 831, 1310, 2358.

Wedes, ⎫ armour, garments, 151,
Wede3, ⎭ 271, 861; foliage of the groves, 508.

Wela-wylle, exceeding lonesome,

desert, 2084. Cf. O.E. *wil-some,*
lonely, desert; *wyl,* astray, for-
lorn.
*Wela-wynne, very joyous, 518.
Welde, possess, enjoy, 835, 837,
1064.
Welde₃, possesses, 1528, 1542, 2454.
We-loo, alas! 2208.
*Wele, wealth, riches, 7, 60, 1270,
1394; joy, 485, 1371, 1767,
2490; good fortune, 997, 2134.
Welkyn, sky, air, 525, 1696.
Welne₃, } almost, 7, 867.
Welne₃e, }
*Wend, } to go, 559, 1028, 1053;
Wende, } went, 90, 1161; gone,
1712.
Wende, thought, 669.
Wende₃, turns, 2152.
*Wene, ween, think, 270, 1226.
Wener, fairer, 945. O.N. *væn.*
O.Dan. *wæn,* beautiful.
Wenged, avenged, 1518.
Went=wend=thought, 1711.
Weppen, weapon, 384.
Werbelande, warbling, whistling,
2004.
Werbles, notes, 119.
Were, wore, 1928.
Were, war, 271; hostility, 1628.
*Were, to defend, ward off, 2015,
2041.
Werned, refused, denied, 1494.
Wernes, denies, 1824.
Wernynge, refusal, denial, 2253.
Werre, war, 16.
Werre₃, make war, 720.
Wesaund, wind-pipe, 1336.
Wesche, washed, 887.
Weterly, savagely, fiercely, 1706.
Weue, to give, 1975.
Weued, gave, 2359.
Wex, waxed, 319.
*We₃ed, carried, 1403.
Wharred, made a whirring noise,
2203.
What, how! lo! 1163, 2203.

What-so, whatsoever, 382, 1550.
Wheder-warde, whitherward, 1053.
Whene, queen, 74, 2492.
Whethen, whence, 871.
Whether, either of two, 203.
Whyrlande, rushing, 2222.
Whyssynes, cushions, 877.
Wich, what, 918.
Wit, } know, learn, 131, 255,
Wyt, } 1508.
Wit, with, 113.
With, } by, 664, 1153, 1229,
Wyth, } 2416.
*Wi₃t, *adj.* great, strong, 1762; *sb.*
strong, fierce (one), 1440.
*Wlonk, fair, beautiful, 515, 581,
1977, 1988, 2432.
Wlonkest, fairest, 2025.
Wod, went, 787.
*Wode, mad with anger, 2289.
Wod-crafte₃, skill in the arts of
the chace, 1605.
Wodwos, wild men, monsters, 721.
A.S. *wudu-wasan,* wood satyrs,
robbers.
Woke (*pret.* of *wake*), watched,
sat up at night, 1025.
Woled=wolde=would, 1508.
Wolde₃, desirest, 2127; wouldst,
2128.
Wombe, belly, 144.
Won, } power or will, or rather
Wone, } possession, 1238; riches,
wealth, 1269. S.Sax. *wunnen.*
*Won, } dwelling, mansion, cham-
Wone, } ber, 257, 736, 906, 2490.
*Won, } to dwell, 257, 814.
Wone, }
Wonde, dwelt. See *Woned.*
*Wonde, to avoid, shrink back,
563.
Wonde, delay, 488.
Wonder, marvel (?), 16. Does it not
rather signify sorrow? S.Sax.
wundre, hurt, mischief.
Wonder, wondrous, 2200.
Wonderly, wondrously, 787, 1025.

Wone, riches, wealth, 1269.
*Woned, dwelt, 50, 701, 721.
*Woneȝ, dwellings, mansions, 685, 1051, 1386, 2400.
*Woneȝ, dwells, 399, 2098.
*Wonnen, conducted, brought, 831; arrived, come, 461, 1365; brought, 2091.
Wont=woned=dwelt, abode, 17. Sir F. Madden renders it use, custom.
Wont, lack, want, 131.
Wont, fail, 987.
Wonteȝ, fails, 1062.
Wonyd, dwelt, 2114.
Wonyes, dwells. See *Woneȝ*.
Worde, fame, reputation, 1521.
Worlde, Nature, 530.
*Wormeȝ, dragons, serpents, 720.
*Worre, worse, 1588, 1591.
Wort, herb, 528.
*Worth, to be, happen, 238, 1202, 1214, 1302; *subj.* be, 2127, 2374.
Worthed, was, became, 485; would be, 2096; become, 678.
Wortheȝ, is, becomes, will or shall be, 2035, 1106, 1387.
Worthe, worthy, 559.
Worthilych, worthy, honourable, 343.
Worthy, worthily, 1477.
Worthy, *sb.* 1276, 1508.
Worthyly, honourably, properly, 72, 144.
*Wot, know, 24.
*Wothe, harm, mischief, injury, 222, 488, 1576.
Wowche-saf, vouchsafe, 1391.
*Wowes, walls, 1180.
Woxes=waxes, grows, 518.
*Woȝe, wrong, harm, 1550.
*Woȝe, wall, 858.
Woȝes, walls, 1650.
*Wrake, destruction, mischief, 16.
Wrast, loud, stern, 1423.
Wrast, advantage (?), 1663. A.S. *wræst*, good.

Wrast, disposed, 1482.
Wrasteleȝ=wrestleȝ, wrestles, 525.
Wrathed, troubled, annoyed, 726.
Wrathed, entangled, ensnared, 2420.
Wreȝande, reviling, 1706. A.S. *wrégan*, to accuse, to drive.
*Wro, obscure corner, 2222.
Wroth,) violent, sharp, boister-
Wrothe,) ous, 70, 319, 525, 1706.
Wroth (*pret.* of *writhe*), moved round, 1200.
Wrothely, angrily, 2289.
Wrotheloker, more angrily, 2344.
Wroȝt,) occasioned, 3, 32.
Wroȝten,)
Wruȝled, clad, folded, 2191.
*Wyghe,) man, knight, 131, 249,
Wyȝ,) 384, 581, 1487; ap-
Wyȝe,) plied to God, 244.
Wykis, corners of the mouth, 1572.
Wylde, used substantively for beasts of the chace in general, 1150, 2003; and in the singular number, 1167, 1586, 1900, the words deer, boar, fox, being respectively understood.
Wyldrenesse, 701.
Wyle,) wily, 1728; used sub-
Wyly,) stantively, 1905.
*Wylsum, wild, desert, and hence unpleasant, 689. O.E. *wyl*, forlorn.
*Wylt=willed, wandered, escaped, 1711.
Wylyde, wild, amorous, 2367.
Wylnyng, will, 1546.
Wyndeȝ, returns, 530.
*Wynne, joy, bliss, 15, 1765, 2420.
*Wynne, goodly, 1032, 2430, 2456.
*Wynne, to come, arrive at, 402, 1537, 2215.
Wynne-lych, cheerful, 980.
Wynneȝ, proceeds, goes, 1569, 2044.
Wynt-hole, wind-hole, 1336.
Wypped, wiped, 2022.